"EUTERPE"

"EUTERPE"

Diaries, Letters & Logs of the "Star of India" as a British Emigrant Ship

Compiled & Edited by Craig Arnold

The Maritime Museum Association of San Diego
San Diego, California
1988

"EUTERPE"

Library of Congress Cataloging-in-Publication Data

"Euterpe" — diaries, letters & logs of the "Star of India" as a British emigrant ship.

    Bibliography: p.
    1. Seafaring life. 2. Euterpe (Ship) 3. Great Britain — Emigration and immigration. I. Arnold, Craig, 1949-
G540.E79 1988   910.4'5   87-28317
ISBN 0-944580-06-8 (pbk.)

Printed and bound in the United States of America
First Printing, 1988
Second Printing, 1994

Published by the Maritime Museum Association of San Diego,
1306 North Harbor Drive, San Diego, California 92101

This work is dedicated to all members of the
San Diego Maritime Museum. With their help,
an iron veteran of the sea lives on.

CONTENTS

ABOUT THE COVER

The cover painting for this book was executed by San Diego marine artist Richard W. DeRosset. It is his conception of the *Euterpe* as she appeared when rounding Cape Horn on January 12, 1885. This rounding was made from west to east during the homeward leg of her "Jonah voyage" of 1884-85.

She has been at sea for nine months—apart from a few weeks at Port Chalmers and Napier—and her "gunport"-painted hull is streaked with rust. Being in rather heavy seas, she carries a reduced suit of sails, and these are braced around to the port tack. According to her log for this voyage, kept by mate William Paterson, she sometimes dropped all "small sail" and scudded along under lower tops'ls alone, with perhaps one upper tops'l set—in this case her fore upper tops'l—for extra driving power. This was far from the most extreme weather she encountered, however.

Three more months till London. Meanwhile the *éminence grise* of Cape Horn keeps watch in the distance, waiting for mariners to make fatal mistakes.

January is the summertime in the Southern Hemisphere—and for the Horn, this day is relatively mild. The ship passes safely on. "Rolling and labouring heavily" she might be—in Mr. Paterson's words—but that is nothing new for the *Euterpe*. She has endured a great deal worse.

ACKNOWLEDGEMENTS

The following persons and institutions have all contributed materially to this book. The author would like to thank:

Captain Harold D. Huycke, Edmonds, Washington
Mrs. Irene Lister, Taradale, Hawke's Bay, New Zealand
Mr. Richard W. DeRosset, La Mesa, California
Miss Jane Abbiss, Wellington, New Zealand
Mr. David Savill, Crowborough, East Sussex, England
Mrs. Doris Trotman, Greytown, New Zealand
The San Diego Maritime Museum, San Diego, California, and its Star of India Auxiliary
The National Archives, Department of Internal Affairs, Wellington, New Zealand
The Tate Gallery, London, England
The National Maritime Museum, Greenwich (London), England
The Philadelphia Maritime Museum, Philadelphia, Pennsylvania
The National Maritime Museum, San Francisco, California

All these persons and institutions were of significant assistance in formulating this work. If anyone has been inadvertently omitted, the author regrets that omission. To all of you, much gratitude.

INTRODUCTION

In the latter half of the nineteenth century, thousands emigrated from the British Isles to all corners of the earth. These were the glory years of the British Empire, the Victorian Age, and the peoples of those islands set out to colonize the globe.

Theirs was one of the greatest migrations of all time, a surging out, a daring leap into the little-known. Abandoning hearths and homes their ancestors had kept for centuries, they boarded frail sailing ships to voyage thousands of miles across forbidding seas, enduring every hardship imaginable. They were jammed like sheep into the 'tween decks and tiny cabins of these vessels. They were poorly fed for the most part, and their drinking water was strictly rationed. (Any laundry or bathing done had to be accomplished with salt water.) Children were born and children died. Sometimes adults died, too—of the dropsy or some other ailment. More often, they were injured by the relentless pitching, rolling, and yawing of the ship as it clawed its way ahead. Seasickness was common, especially in the first weeks of a voyage.

The storms were awful. For weeks they would go "knocking about in the Channel", battling to make westing and clear into the Atlantic. Vast seas deluged the ship, pouring into the 'tween decks and flooding out cabins; even passengers in the saloon were not immune from torrents.

In the tropics, sweltering heat permeated the ship as it drifted through the Doldrums—at times becalmed, when the sea lay flat as glass and not a breath of air came.

In the Roaring Forties below the Cape of Good Hope, the winds returned with a vengeance. If they were bound for Australia or New Zealand, the ship "ran her easting down" here, scudding before the prevailing winds all the way to her destination.

In many ways, this final leg was the ruggedest of all. The ship ran along the northern edge of the Southern Ocean — a cold, bleak, and violent world. Enormous icebergs stretched for miles, the seas rose "mountainous high", as the old logs say. Winds of "hurricane force" could strike out of an "unsettled sky". The pale blue ink of mates inscribing logs speaks of the desperate struggles of men against broken yards, sails blasted away, lines torn loose and gear mangled. A man overboard was a dead man, and most commanders would not lower a boat. Why send others to their deaths for no purpose?

Despite these perils, the emigrants went with high hope and faith in their hearts. The thrill of sighting the new land where they were bound comes through again and again in their writings. And it is by their writings that we know them. In Part One of this book, you will meet some of these people. A few of them kept diaries; others penned detailed letters recalling this experience; still another wrote a long poem — and one even composed a waltz!

The ship these good folk chose to take them to the uttermost end of the earth was the *Euterpe*. Today she is better known by her later name of *Star of India*, and she is kept in first-rate trim by the Maritime Museum Association of San Diego, California.

Euterpe (pronounced yoo-tuŕ-pē) was a small ship, even for that day. Built of iron, she measured 205 feet in length at the waterline and 35 feet in beam. She carried square sails on all three masts — fore, main, mizzen — and her capacity was rated at 1197 tons. (The word "ton," in this sense, meant not the ship's weight or displacement, but was a reckoning of her space for carrying cargo. "Tons" derived from the old English "tuns" — casks of wine stowed in a vessel's hold.)

The ship's name was that of the ancient Greek muse of music and lyric poetry. A figurehead representing the muse gazed out across the waters from her bow.

She was a vessel that had seen years of hard service. Launched in 1863 at Ramsey, Isle of Man, she made six voyages to India in the jute trade — once nearly foundering in a cyclone off Madras. With her sale to Shaw Savill & Co. in 1871, she began a career of hauling emigrants to the lands down under. (She never transported convicts, by the way. Neither had she ever carried slaves or dueled with pirates — contrary to some lurid tales dreamed up many years later.)

The emigrants, of course, were not the only ones on board. There were also the sailors.

Sailoring in Victorian times was something a man did when he couldn't do anything else. It was a brutal, brutish life — apt to be cut suddenly short by a slip aloft or a wave crashing across a bowsprit. For all the danger, however — for all the poor rations, grinding labor and callous treatment — there was a kind of freedom to it. It attracted thousands of young men who had no other prospects. To some, it was better than life ashore had been: setting the royals in the trades beat slopping the pigs back in Yorkshire; and even the toil of off-loading cargo — the most grueling task of all — was no worse than working in a Welsh mine.

The sailors were bossed by the ship's officers, principally the master and mate. One of the mate's many jobs was to keep the ship's log, or record. To the historian, these logs are invaluable. Written in a terse, no-nonsense style, they convey the actual working routine of the ship. They recount the many perils the vessel and her crew had to surmount. They often reveal the personalities of these officers and men.

Taken together, these logs, diaries and other items form a mosaic — a picture of life in *Euterpe*. The purpose of this book is to present this mosaic to the reader in a way that increases his understanding of what these people went through.

For theirs is a great human story. And those among them who created these diaries and other writings realized this. It is thanks to them that we have a picture of life in a Victorian emigrant ship.

For this book we have selected two diaries, four letters, a poem and other items for Part One, entitled "The Emigrants." Part Two, entitled "The Sailors," consists of two logs kept by *Euterpe's* officers on the voyage of 1884. Four voyages are covered in all.

Each voyage is introduced with a brief account of what was going on in the world that year, to place the material in historical context.

The author wishes to thank the San Diego Maritime Museum for making these documents available for his study. He also wishes to thank the Star of India Auxiliary, an arm of the Maritime Museum, for raising funds to make this book possible.

Craig Arnold
Cardiff-by-the-Sea, California
September 1987

Part One:

THE EMIGRANTS

Euterpe as she appeared in her first decade of service with Shaw Savill. The date is April 25th-28th, 1874. The ship is moored in Gravesend Reach, River Thames, just below London. Smoke wafts from "Charley Noble" (the galley stovepipe) as emigrants cluster on her foc'sl head. Richard Cornish and the young Lillian Barry were likely on board at this time. Prior to their merger with the Albion Line in 1882, Shaw Savill painted their hulls dark green. Masts and deckhouses were light brown. The ship's boats, deck fittings and figurehead were white, and her name plus any carved scrolls at bow and stern were done in gold. After the merger, all sailing ships of the combined lines were given new paint jobs in the popular "gunport" style. (Source for painting information: *Sail to New Zealand*, by David Savill)

I.

THE EMIGRANT'S LOT

The first section of this book is devoted to the common emigrants who left their homes in Europe—principally in the British Isles—to voyage halfway round the world to their new homes in New Zealand.

If the average emigrant's lot in steerage was hard, it was often no more so than what he had left. The emigrants on board *Euterpe* came mainly from the working classes of Victorian Britain. They were craftsmen, servants, navvies, millhands and yeomen farmers. Most of the young women were domestic servants—maids, cooks, seamstresses and the like.

As physical specimens, these products of the Industrial Revolution were not impressive. Their work week typically ran to 60 hours or longer; working conditions in factory, farm or counting-house were apt to be both arduous and dismal, and their masters kept them hard at the grindstone. (Domestic servants, for example, commonly had no more than one half-day off per month. They were also allowed to spend a few hours at service every Sunday— there to be subjected to a sermon on "The Virtue of Labour," like as not.)

The diet of the working-class man or woman was notable chiefly for its lack of variety and low nutritional value. Meat, cheese, butter, eggs, and fresh vegetables were often hard to obtain or beyond the means of the city-dweller; while in the countryside, if a crop failed or disease struck the animals, famine might threaten. (This situation was especially bad in the rural areas of Ireland throughout Queen Victoria's reign; added to all other woes, Irish tenant farmers faced the constant threat of eviction, backed up by police. Small wonder that the Irish made up nearly one-third of the emigrants in Shaw Savill ships.)

The class system pervaded all aspects of Victorian Britain. A man of working-class origin could never hope to enter the higher realms of British life, no matter what his talent as an individual. Only out in the rough-hewn colonies and dominions such as Canada, Australia, and New Zealand, was there much opportunity to get ahead.

Whatever his reason for choosing to emigrate—and not all emigrants were badly off—our prospective voyager faced a sharp division of choices right at the start. Ship accommodations were designed around the presumed needs of the various classes. For the fortunate few—not necessarily rich, but comparatively well-off—there was "Chief Cabin" (i.e., First Class). Shaw Savill line's Chief Cabin Fare for the passage to New Zealand ran from £52 to £78. (Equal to £1300 to £1900 at today's values.) For this, the Chief Cabin passenger got a tiny box of a cabin in the saloon area of the ship. This could be purchased for either double- or single-occupancy; single cost more. The passenger had to "furnish" the cabin and provide bedding plus any other creature comforts. Tableware was supplied by the line, and as a special fillup, First Class were allowed an "unlimited table." This meant they got the best of the food including exclusive claim on the livestock. (Their allowance was supposed to be one pig, one sheep, and a dozen ducks and hens per passenger.) Chief Cabin also had steward service at table and in the cleaning of their cabins. All this, and the presumed pleasure of dining with the ship's senior officers.

Second Class wasn't nearly so well off. In the *Euterpe* and

The more fortunate emigrants on board the *Euterpe* had Cabin Class cabins such as this one off the saloon.

other ships, they were normally housed at the after end of the 'tween decks. They had private "cabins" of a sort, flimsy temporary affairs which were knocked down after their departure in the colonies. As with steerage, they had to provide their own bedding, tableware and teapots. Instead of the "unlimited table" of Chief Cabin, they made do with a "Scale of Dietary" which might include soup, York ham, fish, barley and cheese — all of it a notch above what steerage was chewing on. Along with steerage, they formed their own messes, taking rations to the galley for a scorching by the ship's cooks. If the weather was fine, they might dine alfresco on the upper deck. Such was the life of Second Cabin, for which one paid £25 (£624 at today's value).

At the bottom, occupying the most Spartan quarters and subsisting on the least satisfying rations, came the great mass of emigrants. Steerage Berth Fare in Shaw Savill ships ranged from £16 to £20 (£399 to £500 today), depending on whether the berth was open or closed.

(A note here on fares: with the introduction of the so-called "Vogel Scheme" of 1870, followed by the Immigrants Land Act of 1873, the New Zealand Government contracted a passage fare with the shipping companies, and selected emigrants voyaged free to the colony. This was the policy termed "Assisted Immigration"—and it helped account for the country's settlement boom during the 1870s.)

The steerage berths filled up the middle and forward parts of the 'tween decks on board *Euterpe*. It must have been especially hard on the married couples with their children, packed like sardines into the 'midships portion. For good measure, single women were sometimes put in among them if the after end of the deck was taken by Second Class. (Otherwise, the single women of steerage were quartered aft on this deck, with perhaps a few in the saloon. The exact berthing arrangements varied from voyage to voyage, depending on the number and classes of emigrants.)

Steerage had no assistance from the stewards in cleaning their quarters, according to one of their diarists. The forward end of the deck was occupied by the single men, who were separated from the rest by a temporary wooden bulkhead.

Steerage had its own Scale of Dietary. Among the items included were peas, oatmeal, suet, flour, rice, potatoes, carrots and molasses. (A more detailed list of steerage fare is given in Chapter III.) Compared to what some of these people had been getting at home, this may have seemed quite handsome. The rations for all on board were supposed to last 22 weeks and one of the mates kept a sharp eye on this. Usually the rations held out. Sometimes they fell short. When the latter happened, the master tried to put into the nearest port—Rio de Janeiro or Cape Town, perhaps—and re-victual. If the crisis came in mid-ocean—as it once did for *Euterpe*—there might be recourse to the ship's rats.

Fresh water for drinking was yet another worry for all on board. *Euterpe* carried a fresh-water condenser, but on the voyage of 1874 this broke down, with the result that the ship put into Cape Town to repair it. Sea water was used for laundry and any bathing that occurred.

All classes of emigrants were advised by Shaw Savill to bring along various types of clothing suitable for the tropics, the cold of the Southern Ocean, and the rainy country of New Zealand. There were several outfitters in London who specialized in emigrants' wear, most notably Hanning & Co. Shaw Savill limited Chief Cabin passengers to 20 cubic feet of baggage space (free), and charged high rates for anything more. Emigrants were advised by the company not to bring along furniture, but to convert such belongings to cash, then purchase furniture as needed in the colonies. Nevertheless, some of the better-heeled passengers insisted on hauling along their prized heirlooms.

At last all preparations were complete, and the great day of boarding the ship arrived. Most of the emigrants came by train to London or another port, where they were sometimes housed in barracks while their ship was readying to sail. Such accommodations may have been a bruising shock to those used to a quiet country life, but probably helped prepare them for conditions on board ship.

Meanwhile carpenters swarmed over their vessel, hammering together the temporary cabins, berths, and bulkheads. Various inspectors came and went. All sorts of supplies, cargo, and ship's stores were hoisted aboard and carefully stowed. The captain was a busy man, and the mates were working night and day.

Often the first sight of their ship came to emigrants just before boarding, as they crowded into the East India Dock, London; onto a pier at Gravesend on the Thames; or along the teeming banks of the Clyde. "There she is, John!" "There's our ship, Mary!"

There she was, indeed: towering spar upon spar high into the sooty, foggy air; stretching the full length of her sleek green or gunport-painted hull along the pier; or anchored cleanly alone out in the broad reach of the Thames, she was a sight to fill the eye. On her decks and aloft clambered those strange beings called sailors—seeming like monkeys in their agility. Along the pier or quay, horse-drawn wagons jostled for position, the shouts of their drivers mingling with the hawking cries of bummarees and buskers.

For a young farmer from Berkshire or a weaver from the Midlands, this was the most bewildering of worlds. There was a strong smell of tarred cordage, of steam engines, of many cargoes. The East India Dock in particular was a bedlam. The ships were jammed into its rectangular pool so closely that their yards overlapped. (It was a wonder the tugs could work them in and out, and collisions were inevitable.)

Anywhere from 20 to over 400 emigrants might board *Euterpe*. Once on board, trying to settle into their cramped quarters as best they might, they perhaps faced a further delay of several days while the carpenters finished up, the medical inspector made his rounds (reportedly well in his cups on one occasion), a crew was scraped together, and cackling, squealing and snorting livestock were penned atop the main hatch.

Despite all discomforts, the emigrants' spirits were high. All were keyed up to a great adventure. There was singing, chatting, and general horseplay going on late into the night.

At last the tugs arrived and took her out. If there were no collisions and a further delay for repairs (as happened to *Euterpe* in 1875 and 1884), the ship was nosed out into the Thames and towed down the river. Through Woolwich Reach, Gallions Reach, Barking Reach, Erith Rands, Fidlers Reach and Northfleet Hope she went — finally coming to moor in Gravesend Reach, about 20 miles from London. (A "reach" is a stretch between two bends in the river; in olden days a ship could sail a reach without shifting her sails round until she got to the next bend. By *Euterpe's* time, however, large sailing vessels were commonly tugged up and down the river.)

The last few passengers might straggle aboard at Gravesend. These people came out in boats from Town Pier. Sometimes a special ceremony would be held: a band often came aboard to play, a River Missionary gave an uplifting message, and a meal of good food and beer was served. It all helped to fortify any passengers having last-minute doubts.

Another factor which probably steadied many was the high caliber of Shaw Savill's officers. Without exception from the emigrants' accounts we have, the captains and first mates are given the highest marks. It is known that Walter Savill, co-founder and chief executive of the line, devoted much personal attention to the selection of his officers. A skipper had to know his business at sea and in port, and if he committed any blunders, he would have to face Mr. Savill.

Life in the saloon for a ship's Cabin Class passengers had its amenities — including a wood-burning stove for the colder latitudes. This is not *Euterpe,* but a similar ship.

The official that most emigrants came to know best, however, was the Surgeon Superintendent. This man was nominally an employee of Shaw Savill, although he might be working off his passage. His job was to attend to any medical care the emigrants needed, to ensure the cleaning and ventilation of their quarters, and generally to keep an eye on their welfare. At his best, he was a combination of medical doctor, father-confessor, judge over minor disputes, fire-safety inspector, lifeboat-drill supervisor, recreational director, and spokesman for the company to the emigrants. Obviously, to be successful, he had to be a person of forceful character and high moral standards as well as having some degree of medical knowledge. Dr. John Bligh, sailing in *Euterpe* in 1874, was such a man.

His was not an easy task. Disciplinary problems cropped up now and then. Just as the mate kept all hands busy, so the Surgeon Superintendent sought to keep the emigrants occupied. Reading, sewing, diary-keeping and letter-writing were all encouraged — as was participation in concerts, plays, foot races, helping the sailors handle the lines or standing look-outs. (Working the ship could be hazardous for an emigrant, however, as David Savill notes: "On the *Hydaspes* bound for Auckland in 1873, three were knocked overboard when on such work and were lucky to be rescued by the quick reaction of the Commander.")

Then there were outright crimes to be dealt with. The most common of these was theft. Investigations were carried out by the mate, under direction of the captain. Searches of baggage and cabins, and interrogation of suspects, consumed much time and energy that these gentlemen doubtless would have rather spent on something else. If the thief was caught, he would be bound over to a magistrate in the colonies and charges brought against him there — that is, if anyone still wanted to bother with the whole business.

Apart from these rather routine social problems, there were bouts of sickness — starting with a good dose of *mal de mer* for many in the Channel. But Shaw Savill ships in general, and *Euterpe* in particular, seem to have been remarkably free of widespread afflictions. No doubt the rigorous attention of the Surgeon Superintendent to cleaning and airing of quarters, the airing of bedding, and frequent laundry chores for all (in wooden tubs on the main deck) helped. Considering the primitive state of the medical art in those days, it is extraordinary that so few deaths occurred on board ship. Of those who did perish, infants led the list.

These were some of the trials and tribulations faced by the common emigrant. It wasn't all grim, of course. They knew times of joy and formed a lasting bond with those who'd braved the seas with them. On arrival in the colonies, some emigrants wept at having to leave friends made on the voyage. The Victorian was at heart a sentimentalist — and he would commemorate his passage with poetry, testimonials to admired officers, and lifelong memories.

But all that was far away when the ship left Gravesend. The tug took her out of the Thames, round to Deal, and perhaps down the Channel a ways before casting off. Tier upon tier of sails billowed into view, the ship took the wind like a good horse takes the bit, and the voyage had begun. The emigrants lined the rail to catch their last glimpse of England — and at this moment the enormity of their decision must have struck them. The mass would never see the mother country again, nor those they left behind.

What follows, then, is mainly by their own hands.

"The Last of England" by Ford Madox Brown. A picture which hung in many a Victorian home, in which the artist depicted an emigrant family aboard their ship, with the cliffs of Dover dimly visible in the background.

It can be said that the details of the subjects' dress are accurate. Madox Brown had a friend, Thomas Woolner, who sailed from England for Australia. Brown came down to the docks to bid him goodbye, and there sketched the emigrants whom he later immortalized in oils. This work of art illustrates the Victorian attitude toward emigration—a mixture of faith, hope, perseverance and apprehension.

FROM THE PICTURE IN THE TATE GALLERY, LONDON—BY PERMISSION

II.

"INFORMATION FOR INTENDING EMIGRANTS"

The following is extracted from *The Official Handbook of Ocean Travel*, published in London in 1889. One dozen shipping companies — including Shaw Savill & Albion — contributed ads, articles, and advice. The author of the following passages is not credited in the original, but whoever he was, he spoke well to his audience:

MOTIVES TO EMIGRATE.

The first question which a man who thinks of emigrating should ask himself is, "Why should I do so?" And this is perhaps the most important practical question of his life. It means the breaking up of all the old ties and associations of his childhood, and beginning life afresh in a new country, where everything will at first seem new and strange to him. He will, however, in a very short time become familiar with his new surroundings. . . .

It is true that emigration has led to many cases of individual hardship, but these are the exceptions to the rule; and it is a fact that they have nearly always come from the unfitness to emigrate at all of the persons who have suffered. . . .

An intending emigrant should have above all things good health, and be stout-hearted. A man who comes to work should be prepared to do anything at first that comes to his hand; and he should try to adapt himself to the ways of the new country in which he has placed his lot. He may have many things to unlearn, and also to learn, and especially he should learn to follow the practices proved to be wise, by the experience of the new country to which he goes, rather than make any attempt to push them aside by the use of the practices of the Old Country which he has left. This is a truth which men always in the end come to find out, and many have done so through disappointments which might have been avoided. . . .

ADVANTAGES OF EMIGRATION.

There is no subject connected with the happiness and well being of all classes of our over-crowded population of such interest as the all important subject of EMIGRATION. The serious attention of statesmen, philanthropists, and political economists has long been directed towards the most effectual means of relieving the pressure of a population increasing at the rate of 400,000 per annum. Whilst the difficulty of making a living in England is increasing every year, and the public press is teeming with letters from successful emigrants, writing from the land of their adoption, to urge their fellow countrymen, toiling in the over-crowded cities and unproductive agricultural districts of England to follow their example . . . it is now generally admitted that the only practical remedy for poverty, want of employment, and the many evils of an over-crowded country, is EMIGRATION.

Where so many are struggling for every vacant situation, it must needs be, that while one only can be successful, hundreds are left to bear the cold blast of poverty, and although able and willing to work they are doomed to eke out a miserable existence, too often obliged to accept help from some charitable fund, or what is always felt most degrading to the self-respect of the honest working man, to apply for relief from the parish.

There is surely something wrong in this state of affairs.

But apart from the right and wrong of the question, let us ask—what is the remedy? A theme of every day life, namely:—EMIGRATION. . . .

We will now offer to the intending emigrant a few words of advice and information respecting his

LUGGAGE,

and what he should take with him. . . .

Emigrants are recommended to encumber themselves with as little luggage as possible. Articles of furniture and household utensils should *not* be taken, as these can be purchased in [a colony] quite as cheaply as in England.

All large packages of luggage are stowed away in the hold, and, as the passenger is not likely to see them again till the end of the voyage, anything that will be required on the voyage should be put in a small bag or box, marked "Wanted on the Voyage," and taken into his berth. . . .

WHAT TO TAKE.

It is advisable to take out a good supply of woolen clothing and other kind of apparel; but emigrants are warned against the old fallacy of encumbering themselves with *feather beds*. . . .

In taking out

MONEY

it is advisable to obtain a bill of exchange, or a bank-draft for larger sums, as then there is no danger of its being lost. Any smaller sums are better taken in sovereigns, as far as possible, rather than in silver or bank-bills. Even Bank of England bills are subject to the rate of exchange, which may vary, and not always in favour of the emigrant. But gold sovereigns have always their absolute par value. On silver coins, shillings, florins, half-crowns, etc., the emigrant will lose. Take the shilling for instance. Although it freely passes for the $\frac{1}{20}$th of a pound in England, it is not really worth that proportion, it being only what is called a "token," and not a legal tender except for small change. Still, what silver the emigrant takes had better be in shillings. . . .

DURING THE PASSAGE

the emigrant should make himself perfectly familiar with the Rules of the [ship], and should do his best to carry them out. He should pay particular attention to keeping himself clean, as this will tend not only to his own health and comfort, but to that of those around him.

ANY COMPLAINT a passenger has to make should be made to the Captain, who will see that the cause of grievance is removed at once.

NO GRATUITIES are to be paid to Stewards, and if any Steward should so far forget the Company's instructions as to ask a gratuity, he should be promptly reported to the Captain. . . .

And finally, while decrying that enemy to progress — procrastination — let us remind our readers that — "There is a tide in the affairs of men which, taken at the flood, leads on to fortune."

Passengers take the air on the poop deck of a sailing vessel, very like those on board the *Euterpe* did. This Victorian painting by George F. Wright is entitled "Mid-Ocean."

III.

THE VOYAGE OF 1874

1874: A MOMENT IN TIME

The world in 1874 was a steadily shrinking place. All fields were undergoing rapid change, none more so than transportation. On land, railroads stretched their sprawling arms of steel across entire continents. At sea, steamships vied with sail, although the latter — epitomized by such clipper ships as *Cutty Sark* and *Thermopylae* — still held a commanding lead.

Communications were advancing swiftly; distances being whittled down. With speeds that seemed like magic, telegraph messages flashed over thousands of miles. The Suez Canal had been open five years, cutting a voyage from England to India from months to weeks. Also marking its fifth anniversary was the transcontinental railroad across the United States.

Everywhere was written the will to grow. This was the "Gilded Age," the time of unrestrained capitalism. Commerce and industry advanced hand-in-hand to the overthrow of backwardness. The Industrial Revolution was transforming the way people looked and the way they thought; for the first time in history, large numbers of people dressed alike, due to mass-produced clothing. They were enlightened in similar ways, due to mass printings of books and newspapers, and to spreading systems of public education. Finance, politics, and the arts were all bursting with new energy.

In the United States, it was the age of renewed growth after the trauma of civil war. The South was undergoing Reconstruction, with federal troops on hand to enforce it. The North was entering an unprecedented era of commercial and industrial expansion. Even the so-called "Panic of 1873" had failed to cripple business enthusiasm. The illicit practices spawned by rogues like Boss Tweed, Big Jim Fisk and Little Jay Gould could shake but not stop American progress.

In the White House, President Ulysses S. Grant neared the midpoint of his second term. It was not, alas, a happy one. Grant's Vice President, several secretaries of his cabinet, and his son-in-law were up to their silk cravats in corruption. Although Grant himself was not on the take, he would not leave Washington with his once-shining reputation untarnished.

In the West, the frontier surged relentlessly up the long westward slope from the Mississippi River to the Rockies, thence across the Great Basin to the Pacific. "Sodbusters" were moving out on the plains, granted free land by the Homestead Act of 12 years before. In this year, Joseph F. Glidden patented barbed wire, foreshadowing the end of the open range. On the Staked Plains of Texas, the tribes of the southern Cheyenne, the Arapaho, and the Kiowa were being driven to their reservations by the U.S. Army. Newspapers reported pitched battles at Adobe Walls and Palo Duro Canyon. Once this "Red River War" was finished, the Army turned its eyes northward. Lieutenant Colonel George A. Custer and his troops discovered gold in the Black Hills; soon the area was overrun with prospectors, and this guaranteed future trouble with the Sioux.

Meanwhile, what of England and Europe?

England was prosperous and at peace, her growing empire guarded by the Royal Navy and Her Majesty's garrisons in the colonies. If India was the jewel in the crown, the newest lands of promise were Australia and New Zealand. Emigration from the British Isles mounted year by year. At home, Queen Victoria was in the 37th year of her reign; the doughty little widow of Windsor presided over Europe's foremost industrial state. Britain had the best-developed mines and the most efficient railway system in Europe; her merchant marine was far and away the world's largest. Her mills and factories produced prodigious amounts of goods, many of which were shipped overseas.

In politics, Benjamin Disraeli of the Tories ousted his rival, William Gladstone of the Liberals, from 10 Downing Street. "Dizzy" was the Queen's favorite Prime Minister, and he would chart England's affairs for the next six years.

The continent of Europe also experienced peace. For France, however, it was a peace of bitterness and humiliation. Crushed in the Franco-Prussian War of 1870, France had lost her last emperor, Napoleon III; the provinces of Alsace-Lorraine; and her former eminence as the premier military power in Europe. Now she attempted regeneration in the guise of the Third Republic.

The rod that extended over Europe's head now was held by Germany. More correctly, this was the German Empire, the triumphant Second Reich, with its Kaiser Wilhelm I; its "Iron Chancellor," Prince Otto von Bismarck; and its glittering Prussianized army. Sweeping all before a tide of spiked helmets, the Germans had successively beaten Denmark, Austria, and France. What had been a patchwork of small states a decade earlier became, seemingly overnight, a united nation and a portent of darker things to come.

Other major powers were also restless. To the east, the Russian colossus lay under the scepter of Tsar Alexander II. Russia looked to Asia for expansion, with villages fanning out across Siberia all the way to the Pacific. Despite the recent freeing of the serfs, the Russian masses remained sunk in illiteracy, ignorance, and a standard of living lower than any in Europe. The *ukase* of a Tsar and the whips of Cossacks remained their supreme arbiters.

In southeastern Europe and the Near East, the Ottoman Turkish Empire was in decline. The peoples under Turkish rule in the Balkans were on the verge of revolt, supported by their Slavic "brothers," the Russians. The Near East and the desert vastness of Arabia still adhered to the Sultan, but Egypt under her Khedive looked increasingly to the West. The Khedive had brought in English and French engineers, explorers, and army officers to modernize his ancient land. Egypt was even assuming an aggressively imperialistic role, thrusting southward across the Sudan to Khartoum. A British general named Charles Gordon—known as "Chinese" Gordon for his service to the Manchus—was stamping out the slave trade in the Sudan.

Elsewhere in Africa, explorers such as David Livingstone and Henry Morton Stanley were carrying torches into the heart of the Dark Continent. Up the Niger, the Congo, the Zambezi, the Nile and a hundred other rivers they went, hoping to add to geographic knowledge and (sometimes) to convert the heathen. Many of the expeditions were sponsored by the Royal Geographic Society in London. After these trail-blazers came the imperialists. By 1914, nearly the entire continent would be carved into "spheres of influence" by the Europeans.

This then was the shape of things in the year 1874. New forces were at work in the world, tearing down the old—as they always do—and attempting to build up something as yet unknown. Far away from the bustle of Europe and America, remote beyond vast blue seas, lay Australia and New Zealand. Wrapped in a silent cocoon of time stretching backward into prehistory, empty but for the thinnest scatterings of settlers and indigenous peoples, they beckoned to the crowded masses of Europe.

So it was that men, women and children clambered aboard a ship named *Euterpe*, bound for the distant lands.

"A SUMMARY OF EMIGRATION"

The voyage of 1874 was *Euterpe*'s third for the Shaw Savill line. According to the company records, the ship cleared London on April 25th, sailed from Gravesend and Deal on April 28th, and sailed finally from Portland on April 29th. She reached Wellington in New Zealand on August 30th. Her master was Captain Thomas Phillips, a seasoned veteran who had taken her round the world twice before.

Phillips' return to London from his previous voyage in *Euterpe*, on April 8th, had not been the happiest of occasions. According to a note by Phillips, a sailor named Peter Victoor had been sent over the side to paint that day, had tumbled into the Thames, and had been lost. *Euterpe* went on to her berth, and soon began taking emigrants aboard.

The lady in this picture is Selina Euterpe Collingwood (née Robinson), who was born on July 4th, 1874, on board the *Euterpe*. This photo was taken with her family at Wanganui, New Zealand, in 1906. From left to right, they are George Collingwood Jr., George Sr., Eva, Selina Euterpe, and Clifford. Selina Euterpe passed away in 1971. Dr. John Bligh, in the Surgeon Superintendent's Report for the voyage, lists Selina as a daughter of George Robinson (mother's name not given), although he gives her birthdate as July 1st.

PHOTO PRESENTED BY SELINA EUTERPE'S GRANDDAUGHTER,
MRS. DORIS TROTMAN, ON BOARD THE STAR OF INDIA, JULY 4TH, 1987

As she lay at Gravesend on April 27th, a "Summary of Emigration" was carefully made of all the emigrants aboard. This was carried out for the records of the New Zealand Government, which at that time had the policy of Assisted Immigration in effect. This meant that "passage money" was paid to Shaw Savill for each man, woman and child on board to whom the policy applied. On the average, this worked out to between £9 and £16 per person.

The demographics of this voyage are interesting, and may be taken as typical for *Euterpe's* workhorse trips as an emigrant carrier. The Summary gives the following breakdown:

Male Adults	142	
Female Adults	125	
	267	Adults (age 15 and over)
Male Children	66	
Female Children	59	
Infants	17	
	142	Children and Infants
+	267	Adults
	409	"Souls" on board

The four general divisions of labor for men are "Land," "Wood," "Iron & etc.," and "Miscellaneous." Within these divisions, 34 occupations are listed, the largest groups being General Laborers (40), Farm Laborers (23), Blacksmiths (15) and Carpenters (12). Other occupations mentioned include a Constable, "Cowmen," Wheelwrights and a "Navvy."

For the women, "Genl Servants" is the occupation of 28, and there is a sprinkling of cooks and maids, as well as a Seamstress, a Milliner, a Bootcloser and an Upholsteress.

As might be expected, nearly all the emigrants were drawn from the British Isles. These were their nationalities:

English	308	Welsh	12
Irish	63	Italians	4
Scotch	20	Danes	2

From England, the largest numbers came from the counties of Surrey, Middlesex, Hampshire and Kent. From Ireland, County

Tyrone sent more sons and daughters than anywhere else, while Stirlingshire took the palm for Scotland. And there was a single woman from the Isle of Wight.

LILLIAN BARRY

The following is an extract from a letter by Lillian Barry to American historian Harold Huycke, recalling the voyage of 1874:

156 Marine Parade
Napier [New Zealand]
May 10th, 1948

Dear Sir:

In response to your invitation in the Southern Cross for any information regarding the sailing Ship Euterpe: I came from England to New Zealand in that Ship as a child with my parents, leaving England on April 4th, 1874 & arriving at Wanganui N.Z. about August 14th of the same year.[1]

I was too young to remember anything about the voyage, so can only tell you what I have heard my parents & others who came out at the same time have mentioned in my hearing. I was always intensely interested in anything concerning that voyage & the ship & therefore have remembered most of what I have heard, which I am afraid was not very much.

I have heard my parents say how closely they were crowded, the married people & small children all in together & the only privacy being a curtain in front of their bunks. The single girls were in the part of the vessel called the poop & they were all gathered together after the evening meal by the Chaperone in charge of them & not allowed out again till next morning. The food at times was very bad & once when a complaint was made

---

[1]According to a history of the Abbiss family, who also emigrated on the voyage of 1874, the ship docked at Wellington. This agrees with company records, which state that the ship arrived at Wellington on August 30th after a passage of 127 days, port to port. However, the Abbisses believe that some passengers went on to Wanganui. Among these could have been Lillian and her family.

regarding the soup, an investigation revealed a man's Marino sock in the stock pot.

There was a child born on the voyage, he was named William Euterpe Gibbs. There was also a death on board but I do not know any details. I remember my Father telling me that an Albatross alighted on the deck of the Ship & it measured 22 feet from wing tip to wing tip. Also they were becalmed for a fortnight, somewhere about the Cape of Good Hope.

Quite a number of the emigrants settled in a place called Bulls, among them being a Mr. & Mrs. Armstrong, one of whose sons later became a Cabinet Minister in the first Labour Government, & whose grandson is the present M.P. for Napier.

I have often wondered what became of the Euterpe, as I have never seen her mentioned anywhere & was thrilled to read about her in the Southern Cross. We had a big green sea chest in our home with the name Euterpe in large white letters across the top & as a child I used to trace those letters with my finger & spell the name.

Yours very sincerely,
(Mrs.) Lillian Barry

"WITH REGARD TO THE NECESSARY OUTFIT . . ."

Shaw Savill urged prospective emigrants to equip themselves as follows (taken from *New Zealand and Its Resources*, a book published by the line in 1863):

Mattrasses (which should be new, if possible, and of the following dimensions: — for men, 6 feet by 20 inches; Women, 5 feet 9 inches by 18 inches; Married Couples, 6 feet by 3 feet; Children, according to size), Bolsters, Blankets, and Counterpanes, Canvas Bags, to contain Linen, &c.: Knives, Forks, Spoons, Metal Plates, Hook Pots, Drinking Mugs, Water Can, &c. Also, necessary clothing as under, viz.: —

FOR MALES.

6 Shirts.
6 Pair Stockings.
2 Warm Flannel or Guernsey Shirts.
2 Pair New Shoes.
2 Complete Suits Strong Exterior Clothing.

FOR FEMALES.

6 Shifts.
2 Warm and Strong Flannel Petticoats.
6 Pair Stockings.
2 Pair Strong Shoes.
2 Strong Gowns, one of which must be warm.

FOR CHILDREN.

7 Shirts or Shifts.
4 Warm Flannel Waistcoats.
1 Warm Cloak, or Outside Coat.
6 Pair Stockings.
2 Pair Strong Shoes.
2 Complete Suits of Exterior Clothing, and a
   sufficient supply of covering for the head.
   Also, 3 sheets for each berth, and 4 towels
   and 2 lbs. Marine Soap for each person.

"THE VOYAGE OF THE SHIP EUTERPE"

This poem by a *Euterpe* passenger, Richard Cornish, is presented here as it appeared from a Feilding, New Zealand, print shop in 1874. Mr. Cornish was no Kipling; his meter limps and his meaning is sometimes unclear. Nonetheless, his poem conveys something of the voyage's facts as well as the emigrants' spirit. These verses were recited at a concert given at the end of the voyage, and dedicated to his fellow passengers by the author:

On April the eighth and twentieth day,
This statement is true, I am now going to say,
We left the shores of England, which looked so gay,

As the moon sank down with its beautiful ray.
Our anchors we weighed, as sailors join in their song,
To start a long voyage, just sixteen thousand miles long.

The saloon of *Euterpe*. Captain Thomas Phillips, Dr. John Bligh, and many other Euterpeans dined here. Note racks on teak dining table, to keep dinnerware from going "galley west" in a gale.

Friends stand on the shore, and watch as they might,
We are lost to their vision and soon out of sight.
The English Channel in two days we left,
Still trusting in Him who supplies us with breath,
And crossing the Bay of Biscay so deep,
Where the crew of the London is commanded to sleep.

With fair wind and weather we advanced to the Line,
Where the sun in its splendour forgets not to shine;
The Tropics we crossed, permit me to make mention,
Where flying fishes with others attracted our attention.
A vessel sailed near us, by the side of us stayed;
Sweet Home was the song on a cornet one played.

Albatrosses and pigeons flew around and around,
Again a vessel in hailing said, "Where are you bound?"
She quickly passed by, nor with us did stay;
We replied "To the Cape, then in Wellington Bay."
Soon we sighted Mount Table,[2] and on it did we stare
As it majestically stood towering up in the air.

As we sailed near the shore, and looked on the sand,
The clouds o'er the mountains looked awfully grand;
On the top of some mountains, though be it a mystery,
Are the grandest events ever recorded in history.
We reached Simon's Town through much tribulation,
And glad to cast anchor to take up our station.

On July fourth we were filled with delight,
On a Saturday morning to see such a sight:
There were houses before us, though not quite in a row,
Yet they looked just as white as if covered with snow,
Ships lying near us prepared for the slaughter,
And a man cut his throat on board the Shirewater.[3]

A dreadful occurrence, we cannot but think,
Now take my advice and don't touch strong drink.
We took in supplies, then went on our way,
Directing our course for Wellington Bay.
The weather soon changed as we looked on the deep,
The waves lifted up their heads and the waters did leap.

They seemed to play with each other, to wrestle,
And some were so bold as to leap in the vessel;
Tin cans and tubs, mind it is not a delusion,
Rolled around on our decks in utter confusion.
The weather was such that it often did vary,
A little while fine, but it soon got contrary.

---

[2]I.e., Table Mountain at the Cape of Good Hope.

[3]Cornish refers to H.M.S. *Shearwater*, a wooden screw sloop then at Simonstown.
Her Chief Engineer repaired *Euterpe's* water condenser.

But to the wind and weather we must bow in submission.
I have now to record a most solemn addition:
George Walters, a youth in the Warspite was trained,
In the Euterpe he embarked to sail over the main;
Dependant on Him who supplied him with breath,
But he soon had to fall by the cold hand of Death.

A sail stack on the mainmast. From the bottom up, the sails are the mains'l,
lower main tops'l, upper main tops'l, main topgallant, and main royal. The fore
and mizzen masts of *Euterpe* carried the same square sails. At her main truck,
Shaw Savill's house flag dances jauntily over all.
PHOTO COURTESY OF ROBERT SHARP (TAKEN AT SEA, NOVEMBER 11TH, 1984)

He fell from the boom and sank in the wave,
Let us trust that Jehovah was mighty to save;
It was a warning from God to be prepared quite,
As death comes like a bear or a thief in the night.
Birds came to greet us, glad tidings they brought,
They dropped on the yard arms, but were instantly caught.

They were not overfat nor yet very poor,
But a very bad welcome from the Wellington shore.
Children's deaths we had two, six children being born,
The youth I have said we have his loss to mourn.
Some come in the world, others go out of time,
So it was with our crew of four hundred and nine.

We entered Cook's Straits and fired a gun,
We sent up the rockets and the brilliant light shone;
The Pilot commanded for the anchor to strike
On August the thirtieth on a Sunday night.
The waters we passed, and quite thankful to He,
Who all things controlleth, both the wind and the sea.

Officers and sailors have our very best wishes,
We are glad to near land, to pack up our dishes;
Then hurrah for our captain, let us wish him good speed,
May he be a good Christian sailor in word and in deed.
Let us all thank our God and that Being adore,
Who preserved us in crossing to the Wellington shore.

"PASSENGERS' CONTRACT TICKET"

Passengers like Richard Cornish may well have been dismayed
at their first reading of this contract, issued prior to departure
from England. In it were set down the terms of transport from
England to New Zealand, as stipulated for the Assisted Immigration policy.

A typical contract was issued to a family of four, the
Footheads—Edward J. (24); Thirza (25), young son Arthur E.
(2); and "Infant" James F. (presumably under 2). At least no one
spun any webs of illusion for these people; if conditions of passage
were to be Spartan in the extreme, this was set forth plainly. The
total cost to the New Zealand Government of shipping the
Footheads halfway around the world came to £36, 5s. — and every
penny would be accounted for. In a rolling script that seems to
anticipate the rolling main, an official named Sutherland filled
in these particulars:

"EUTERPE" of 1197 Tons Register, to take in passengers at East India Dock London for Wellington New Zealand, the Twenty-first day of April 1874. I engage that the person named in the margin hereof shall be provided with a Steerage Passage to, and shall be Landed at, the Port of Wellington in the Province of Wellington New Zealand, in the Ship "Euterpe" with not less than Ten Cubic Feet for baggage for each Statute Adult, and shall be victualled during the voyage and the time of detention at any place before its termination, according to the subjoined Scale, for the sum of £36 5s. including Government dues before embarkation, and head money, if any, [illegible] place of landing, and every other charge except Freight for excess of Luggage beyond the quantity above specified, and I hereby pledge to have received the sum of ________ in part/full payment.

The final words after "sum of" were crossed through to indicate that the colonial government was picking up the tab.

Lest anyone be misled by that bit about "victualled during the voyage," the framer of this document went on to describe the emigrant's bill of fare:

The following quantities, at least, of Water and Provisions (to be issued daily) will be supplied by the Master of the Ship, as required by Law, viz., to each Statute Adult Three Quarts of Water daily, and an additional Quart of Water daily while the Ship is within the Tropics, exclusive of what is necessary for cooking the articles required by the Passenger Act, to be issued in a cooked state, and a Weekly Allowance of Provisions according to the following Scale: —

Scale of Dietary for each Adult Passenger per Week.

ARTICLES.	Steerage.	
Preserved Meats	1½	lb.
Salt Beef	1½	”
Salt Pork	1	”
Biscuit	3½	”
Flour	3	”
Rice or Oatmeal	1½	”
Peas	½	pint
Sugar, raw	1	lb.
Tea	1½	oz.
Coffee	2	”
Butter	6	”
Molasses (W. India)	½	lb.
Raisins	½	”
Suet	6	oz.
Pickles	¼	pint
Mustard	½	oz.
Pepper	½	”
Salt	2	”
Potatoes, Fresh, or	2	lb.
Ditto Preserved	½	”
Water	21	quarts
Lime Juice (while in Tropics)	6	oz.

Children between one and four years of age to receive preserved meat, instead of salt meat, every day; and in addition to the articles to which they are entitled by the above-written scale, a half pint of preserved milk daily, and every alternate day one egg or two table spoonfuls of condensed egg, and 4 ozs. of arrowroot or sago weekly. Children under one year old, 3 pints of water daily; and if above four months old, half a pint of preserved milk daily, and every alternate day one egg or two table spoonfuls of condensed egg; also 3 ozs. preserved soup, 12 ozs. biscuit, 4 ozs. oatmeal, 4 ozs. sago or arrow root, 8 ozs. flour, 4 ozs. rice, and 10 ozs. sugar weekly.

These meticulous, minute measurements were all part of the requirement for strict rationing on long voyages. Children counted as one-half of one "Statute Adult"—therefore, the Footheads with one child (infants didn't count for standard rations) received 2½ times the weekly ration.

It wasn't any feast. But these were working-class Victorians, for the most part; they neither sought nor expected luxurious treatment. They lived in an age when children were commonly sent to the mines or mills at ages of 10 or under, when infant death was commonplace.

Even so, and despite their apparent variety, these rations were scarcely conducive to proper nutrition.

"Preserved meats," for example: In the days before refrigeration, this meant meat preserved by pickling or heavy salting. Most commonly, the "preserved" aspect was more apparent in labeling than in taste, and the meat was often spoiled before much time at sea.

"Salt Beef" and "Salt Pork": This meat, bathed in brine for months on end, was commonly referred to as "salt horse" and "salt junk" by the sailors. Drawn from casks, it constituted their standard meat ration from the days of King Henry VIII to the advent of modern refrigeration. In the *Gwydyr Castle*, a British bark sailing to Panama in 1901, Anton Otto Fischer recalled salt horse that "looked exactly like a colored chunk of wood and was of about the same consistency. To prove our point, I produced a ship's model I had whittled from the first piece."

"Biscuit": This almost certainly meant "sea-biscuit," often called "hardtack." It was nothing but unleavened bread, straight and flat and hard as sheet-iron, a challenge to the teeth and the digestive tract alike.

The rest of the items furnished, in the cheeseparing manner of the time, are self-explanatory. A special mention might be made of two items: The molasses was doled out with a fairly generous hand because it came cheap from the British West Indies. (Better employed, the cane sugar of those islands went into the making of fiery rum that was the daily "tot" of the Royal Navy.)

The lime juice ration was important to the prevention of

scurvy. Terms like "Vitamin C" were unknown then — but sailors back to Captain Cook took care to provision their ships with adequate quantities of citrus to ward off an especially wasting disease. (Hence the nickname "Limey" for a British sailor.)

Shaw Savill advised emigrants to take along their own foodstuffs to supplement or enhance the rations — jams, jellies, "ordinary fancy biscuits" and "preserved milk" were recommended. Liquor could be purchased from the stewards, but the quantity consumed by all was regulated by the captain. Shaw Savill sold port and sherry wines, ale and porter, and "spirits" (the latter being available to Chief Cabin only). No private stocks of liquor were allowed.

In sum, the common emigrant was "victualled" not much better than the common sailor of the time. The obvious testament to his toughness is that he endured this diet with good cheer, and went on to tame a raw new country.

IV.

THE VOYAGE OF 1874: POSTMORTEMS

After the voyage, the following reports were made by Immigration Commissioners and the Surgeon Superintendent, Dr. John Bligh, to the Minister of Immigration for the colony of New Zealand. Dr. Bligh made the voyage of 1874 in *Euterpe*, while the Immigration Commissioners inspected the ship at Wellington. The two reports are published here in their entirety.

Reference is often made in these reports to "Statute Adults." An adult counted as one statute adult, a child as one-half of a statute adult, and infants were either counted as one-quarter of an adult, or not counted at all. (There seems to have been some discrepancy in the latter category, the Immigration Commissioners hewing to the one-quarter formula and Dr. Bligh not using it.) These reckonings were made for the New Zealand Government's policy of assisting immigrants. The number of statute adults determined the amount of assistance paid.

The author wishes to make special acknowledgment to the National Archives, Wellington, N.Z., for making these documents available for publication.

THE IMMIGRATION COMMISSIONERS' REPORT

"Euterpe"
Commrs Report

Wellington, 7th Sept. 1874.

Sir,

We have the honour to report the arrival of the Ship "Euterpe" on the 30th Ultimo with 330½ Statute Adults including one stowaway whose parents were on board. There were 2 deaths equal to ½ an adult and six births during the voyage. Early on the 31st we inspected the Ship and Immigrants and were pleased to find the people so well and contented after their long voyage of 123 days.

The Single women were berthed partly in the Saloon and partly in the tween decks, the entrance to their compartment being the

"The State Room" — a Victorian woodcut of what a first-class passenger might find aboard ship. Note the washbasin. In the *Euterpe,* one had to furnish any such creature comforts by oneself. Only bunks and tableware (for first class) were furnished by the line.

SOURCE: KARL KORTUM, NATIONAL MARITIME MUSEUM, SAN FRANCISCO

after gangway near the wheel. This we consider a very great improvement as it obviates the necessity of the girls going on the main deck to reach their compartment. The Hospital, Bathroom and water closet, were good, and the compartment was clean and well ventilated. The matron seemed to be well suited for her work and was highly spoken of by the Surgeon Superintendent and Captain.

The Single men had a comfortable, clean and well lighted compartment forward.

The married people were in the middle of the vessel. This compartment was also in good order, the hospital was an exceedingly convenient one under the poop.

The only thing we have to condemn in this vessel was the position of the dispensary; with reference to which we would direct attention to the remarks of the Surgeon Superintendent which are appended hereto. The Galley was convenient and well suited for the requirements of the passengers, but we were informed that the condenser could not make a sufficient quantity of water to enable the passengers to have their daily allowance in full. The Captain therefore very wisely decided upon calling at Simon's Bay for a supply of water.

The Immigrants seem to be a fine healthy lot of people and on being questioned they stated they had no complaints whatever to prefer.

In conclusion we recommend the payment of all gratuities and we consider that Captain Phillips and Surgeon Superintendent Bligh have faithfully performed the duties entrusted to them.

We append Summary of the voyage by Dr. Bligh to which we would direct your attention.

> We have the honour to be Sir,
> Your Obedient Servants
> Alexander Johnston, M.D.
> H.J.H. Eliott
> John Holliday   Commissioners

THE SURGEON SUPERINTENDENT'S REPORT

Ship "Euterpe"
August 28th 1874

Sir,

In accordance with my instructions received from the Agent General for New Zealand in London, I embarked on board the Ship "Euterpe" on the morning of the 24th of April. The passengers were all taken in the same morning and properly berthed for the night. The ship hauled out of the East India Docks next morning, and anchored at Gravesend in the evening, having been detained at Greenhithe, sometime, adjusting compasses. We lay at our anchorage until Tuesday morning, when, having been duly inspected by the Emigration Officers and the New Zealand Despatching Officer, we were towed down the river to the Downs.

We made a rapid passage down Channel and discharged our pilot off Portland on the 29th. Thence to the line we had a very favorable run, accomplishing the distance in 29 days. In crossing the Doldrums we were fortunate enough in not encountering any decided calms.

After passing through the S.E. trade winds, it was found that the condenser was not making the required quantity of water and that the coals expended were so out of proportion with that produced, that Captain Phillips, after an earnest consultation with me, decided upon putting into Simon's Bay and refilling the ship's water tanks. Having encountered baffling winds and having had some very rough weather, we succeeded in beating up False Bay and anchoring in Simon's Bay, about daybreak on the 5th of July. When a sufficient supply of water was taken on board and the condenser surveyed by the Chief Engineer of H.M. Dockyard & the chief engineer of H.M.S. "Shearwater," we put to sea again on the 7th. From the Cape of Good Hope to the coast of New Zealand, the passage has been greatly prolonged owing to a succession of gales & Easterly winds.

The following appointments were made before and since the ship left Gravesend. The Matron and schoolmaster were selected by the Agent-General, but the others picked out by myself as occasion demanded.

Matron
Mrs. Sarah Ann Boddy
Jane Bosher (assistant matron, in charge of children's school)

Surgeon's Assistant
Richard Longmore

Nurse
Mary Wapland

Constables

For the Single women
James Jones
Louis Baker

For the Single men
Henry Taylor
James Clark

For the Married people
Joseph Wallis
Alfred Box

Deck Constable
John Prendergast

Special Constable in charge of Water Closets
Richard Williams

Cook's Assistant
Thomas Horne

Schoolmaster
James McMurrin

I believe that the various offices, for which the persons, just mentioned, have been appointed, were performed efficiently and well. I can, therefore, recommend the holders of them for the usual gratuities. The matron I have always found reliable and trustworthy in every respect. Whilst she has been kind and considerate in her treatment of those committed to her care, she has never failed to maintain proper discipline with quiet firmness. To her, must be attributed in full measure the success which I consider has attended the management of the Single Women's Department.

The assistant matron was appointed for the purpose of looking after the younger children and conducting a school in the Department, when they were unable to attend on deck. She has conducted this school with great ability and success, without any view to remuneration. The progress of the children has been so marked, that I sincerely hope it may be consistent with the interests of the New Zealand Government, to grant her a gratuity as she thoroughly deserves it.

The duties performed by the Constables for the Single Women's Department have, owing to the severe weather, been arduous in the extreme. If the Government would mark their appreciation of their conduct by an increased gratuity, it would be well deserved.

Mr. Longmore has always performed his duties to my entire satisfaction. In education and unobtrusive gentlemanly behaviour, I have never found him wanting. I cannot speak too highly of his character in all respects.

I have from time to time, during the voyage, made myself acquainted with the quality of the provisions & water served out to the Emigrants. These as a rule, have been very good. Whenever, through any accident, one or other of them has been bad, I have invariably ordered a fresh supply. The cooking has not always been performed as well as might be desired, but when the number of passengers and the severity of the weather are taken into consideration, I do not think that the shortcomings of the cook were much greater than those of his class on shore. Whenever a direct charge was brought against him, of shorting food, I invariably investigated the matter, and ordered the materials to be replaced in those cases in which I thought him to blame.

The various paragraphs of the Queen's Order in Council which relate to the airing of bedding and the maintenance of cleanliness on the 'tween decks have been as thoroughly carried on as circumstances and weather would admit. To this, I think, may be ascribed in a great measure, the immunity from severe illness, that has attended a long and difficult passage. Only two deaths have occurred since starting and these in two constitutionally delicate children. The following is a copy from the official Log.

"May 14th 1874. 4.00 P.M. Lat. 25.30 N. Long. 24.20 W. Albert E. Saunders, aged 5 months, son of Edwin C. and Mary A. Saunders, died this day from Infantile Diarrhoea and exhaustion/ hand fed/and was buried at 6.30 P.M."

This child was brought up from birth on the bottle and was very ailing in consequence.

"May 24th 1874. 0.10 A.M. Lat. 3.44 N. Long. 23.0 W. Esther M., aged 3 years, daughter of Henry and Esther Bosher, died in the course of the night from Infantile Diarrhoea & congestion of the lungs and was buried at eight o'clock, this morning."

The child was weak from birth and had undergone an operation at St. George's Hospital, London, a short time before leaving England.

Six births have occurred on the passage & both the mothers and infants have done well.

The school was held with regularity, up to the time of putting into Simon's Bay. Since that time the weather has been too severe to allow of its being held on deck. And I was opposed to its being held in the 'tween decks, not considering it possible in this crowded state, to allot space for it. Miss Jane Bosher has, however, conducted a school in the single women's department for the younger children & the girls between the ages of 12 & 15. This school has proved a decided success.

The conduct of all on board has been as a rule extremely good and I do not consider it necessary to bring before your notice any case of bad behaviour or insubordination, with the exception of one. This is where, five passengers, who had paid their passages refused to do any part of the scraping but that in front of their bunks. As their general behaviour has been good, I hope a severe reprimand will be considered sufficient, without entering a prosecution against them on arrival.

The drugs I have found good, and the medical comforts abundant. The Dispensary, however, was as inconvenient and uncomfortable as could have been devised. It was totally destitute of ventilation and very nearly so of light, the latter being only admitted through a small dead light in the deck above. In the tropics, it was as hot but considerably more relaxing than the calidarium of a Turkish Bath. In rough weather or when the decks were crowded it was impossible to see sufficiently to perform the simplest minor surgical operation. A Dispensary on the upper deck or in one of the cabins which open on the main deck, would be very much to be preferred.

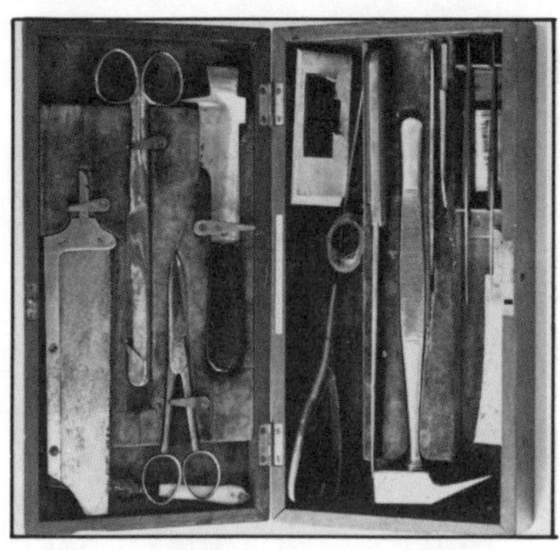

A surgical kit from the Victorian period, similar to what Dr. John Bligh probably carried on the voyage of 1874. Its contents include a bone saw (most surgeries were amputations), a clamp, several probes, a hammer, a large needle for large ligatures, and ivory-handled forceps. With these implements, simple surgical procedures such as amputations and the probing of injuries could be performed.

In closing this, my report, allow me to place on record my sincere thanks to the Captain and officers of the ship "Euterpe," for the kindness and consideration they have invariably shown those under their care, as well as for the ready and willing assistance they have always given me.

I am, Sir,
Your obedient Servant
John W. Bligh, M.D.
Surgeon Superintendent

Synopsis

	Actual Adults	Children	Infants	Souls	Statute Adults
Single Women's Department	56	7	0	63	59½
Married People's Department	138	118	17	273	197
Single Men's Department	80	0	0	80	80
Total taken on board	274	125	17	416	336½

Increase

Births.

On the 9th of May, the wife of Cecil Stoom, of a son.
On the 12th of May, the wife of William Pitts, of a son.
On the 1st of July, the wife of George Robinson, of a daughter.
On the 17th of July, the wife of Richard Williams, of a son.
On the 6th of August, the wife of Isaac Gibbs, of a son.
On the 13th of August, the wife of Charles Pearson, of a daughter.

Stowaway

James Bolger.

Deceased.

On the 14th of May, Albert E. the infant son of Edwin E. Saunders
On the 24th of May, Esther M., the daughter of Henry Bosher, aged 2 years

Insane

Annie, the wife of David Simpson

V.

THE VOYAGE OF 1875-76:
JOHN GRIFFITHS

1875-76: A MOMENT IN TIME

These years were fairly peaceful ones. Europe was calm, despite the fact that Russia was girding for war with Turkey. This broke out in 1877, with the rest of the continent looking on. Most of the conflict would take place in the Balkans. When it was over, the new nations of Rumania and Serbia (the southern part of what is now Yugoslavia) emerged from the rubble. The power of the Sublime Porte receded to a narrow strip along the Aegean, and Russia gained Slavic allies on the southern flank of the Austro-Hungarian Empire.

Britain was concerned about Russian expansion in a different part of the world — India. The British Raj was now separated from Russian Central Asia only by the primitive buffer state of Afghanistan. The Afghans were no pushovers, however; the British had had a taste of war with them in the 1840s, and had gotten the worst of it. Still, the area bore watching as the Russian bear stretched its paws down from the north. Prime Minister Disraeli set about reinforcing India, and a number of regiments filed aboard troopships in English ports, their bands blaring "Nellie Bly" and "The Girl I Left Behind Me."

In America, it was time to mark a birthday—the first hundred years of the republic. The main party opened in Philadelphia, at the Centennial Exposition. American science and industry displayed their newest wares: George H. Corliss's giant stationary engines, an improved mechanical reaper, and a host of other implements and gadgets. Most startling of all, however, was a small, simple-looking instrument invented by one Alexander Graham Bell. On the first day of the Exposition, the Emperor Dom Pedro of Brazil held the instrument to his ear and listened. "My God, it talks!" he exclaimed. The telephone had been born.

Elsewhere in the United States, things were a bit less festive. The South endured the final years of Reconstruction—an era marked by mob violence, political turmoil, night riders and all-too-frequent lynchings. At Baton Rouge, Louisiana, a pitched battle took place in the statehouse between black and white legislators. Federal troops brought the house to order at bayonet-point.

In the West, the Army was on the warpath against the Sioux and northern Cheyenne tribes of Montana and Wyoming. Early results were disastrous for the "white eyes," however: the Sioux emerged victorious at Powder River, Rosebud Creek, and the Little Bighorn. A later engagement at Slim Buttes, Dakota Territory, and subsequent skirmishes saw the Indian coalition falling apart under relentless pressure. By the spring of 1877, most of the Sioux had either surrendered or fled to Canada.

In American politics, President U.S. Grant was under fire from his horde of foes. Buffeted by the Belknap Affair, Credit Mobilier, and other scandals, Grant would not be nominated for a third term. Instead, the Republicans chose Rutherford B. Hayes, congressman from Ohio. Hayes had a good Civil War record and a wife called "Lemonade Lucy"—a religious woman who would try to ban alcohol from the White House. (Her servants got around this by spiking the oranges served for dessert with rum.)

Hayes's opponent in the 1876 election was Governor Samuel

J. Tilden of New York. Tilden actually won the popular vote, but a last-minute switch of votes in the Electoral College threw the job to Hayes. (This switch was greatly aided by a massive voiding of Tilden ballots and bribery.)

So the world spun on. Emigration from Europe to the four corners of the earth continued to swell. Again the *Euterpe* would "set sail from London Town" with a shipload of people eager to start new lives on the opposite side of the globe.

VICTORIAN LONDON: BUSTLE AND TRANQUILLITY

London was *Euterpe's* home port and point of most frequent departure when she sailed for the Shaw Savill line. In the late Victorian era, the great city thrummed with commercial and cultural activity. Some of the flavor of this is conveyed in these paintings by A. Barraud, C.E. Flower, and other artists of the time. Many emigrants who boarded the *Euterpe* must have been familiar with these sights.

Horse-drawn buses clatter along at Charing Cross. Note passengers riding in the tops—an arrangement later carried on with the more familiar motorized buses.

Cheapside — swarms of pedestrians and more horse-drawn buses.

Hyde Park. Two artists capture the glories of nature.

The Library, Inner Temple.

The Imperial Institute. Such arabesque piles of stone and reddish brick were typical of Government buildings from Belfast to Bombay.

Hansom cabs at Leicester Square. The Empire Theatre is in the left background, the Alhambra to the right.

JOHN GRIFFITHS AND THE *EUTERPE*

This voyage followed that of Lillian Barry and Richard Cornish. Once more Captain Thomas E. Phillips was in command, and once more *Euterpe* cleared from the Thames and sailed through the English Channel, sailing finally from Plymouth on January 2nd, 1876.

She reached Port Lyttelton, the port for Christchurch on South Island, New Zealand, on April 11th, 1876. A faster passage was recorded for this trip: 119 days port to port (99 land to land) versus a plodding 127 days the previous voyage.

On the return to England, she departed Lyttelton June 30th, bowled east through the "Roaring Forties" toward Cape Horn, rounded it during the Southern Hemisphere's winter, and stood on up the Atlantic to London. She arrived back in the Empire's capital on October 8th. (*Euterpe* would use this homeward route repeatedly during her years with Shaw Savill. Occasionally, she varied it by sailing up to San Francisco, or touching at Chilean ports, before rounding the Horn.)

John Griffiths was a young steerage passenger on the outward leg of this voyage, another emigrant of meager means seeking a better life abroad. Despite a very indifferent attitude toward spelling and punctuation, he was able to keep a remarkable diary. We publish it with some punctuation added to improve clarity, but with the original spelling intact in order to preserve its flavor.

THE JOHN GRIFFITHS DIARY, OR "ON BORD THE EUTERPE TO NEWZEALAND"

We left London Tuesday December the 14th 1875 about 11 Oclock in the morning. We came out of the docks and down the river very steady with out any damage. We had to ancour about half way down to Gravesend on acount of the fog which was very thick; the fog bell was ringing all the time.

We weighed ancour about middle night and went to Gravesend; we took one or two passengers on bord there. We had a stir-up about four Oclock in the morning; there was a rat got in the young ladies burth and theay screamed murder. We did not know what was the matter; we thought there was something the matter with the ship untill we went to see.

We left Gravesend about two Oclock; we went down for a few Hours, then had to ancour again. The fog came on so thick we could not see anything before us. The fog bell rung at interveals for about 40 Hours; we were at a standstill all that time. We weighed ancour about 10 Oclock friday morning as the fog cleared away. We had a fine night after.

We past Deal, the Foland Lights[1] and Dover. The Pilot was with us all the time. About two Oclock Satuurday morning the tugboat left us. We had one pilot on bord still; he will not leave us till we are at Start Point.

------

[1] I.e., the lights of South Foreland, between Deal and Dover.

We are getting it rather rough to-day Sunday; we are all rather sickley and are preparing for a storm. We are passing the isle of White.[2] It is splended for aneyone who as never been on the water before—that is if theay have aney taste for sea-going sights.

Monday 20th December 1875. We had a very bad job on bord this morning: One of the salloon passengers named Capt. MacBarnett comitted seuicide by cutting his throte in his bunk while in the orrers.[3] He did it a little before breakfast in the morning. It as put a gloomie appierance on the ship. They brought him out of the bunk and put him on the main atch to wait the inquest. The captain and passengers eld the enquest and twas brought in that he was ensaine when he done it. He was sowed up in a piece of sailcloth and burried in about four Hours after he had don it. It was a fearful sight to see the blood all over the place after fetching him out.

The sceremonies was very oppressive seeing the sailors and passengers with their hats and caps off and the captain reading the burial over the corps before puting it down into the water. It put a damper on the whole ship.

From the 20th to 24th we had rough wether. The 25th Christmas day very calm and fine which was appreciated very much after aving such rough times of it. We are still in the Channel.

Christmas night there was a jolly spree; there was a lot of them drunk on bord. We were all sober in the third class; we had only two bottles of wine in our cabbin. There was dancing on deck. We had a banjo and fiddle and a concertina. We were all up till about 11 Oclock.

The sailors and saloon passengers and second cabbin passengers were all about drunk but the Captain was quite sober.

---

[2] I.e., the Isle of Wight.

[3] It is possible that the phrase "in the orrers" conveys an old English expression, "in the horrors"—meaning delirium tremens.

This memo written by Superintendent Joseph Watson to the Register General
of Seamen discusses two deaths in *Euterpe* on the voyage of 1875-76.

SOURCE: NATIONAL MARITIME MUSEUM, LONDON, U.K.

We were very glad to see him so. You see it was quite calm or i dont think we should of had such a spree because we were in a very daingrous place if it had been rough wether.

I shall never forget my first Christmas day at sea. We all enjoyed ourselves very much. Me and father had apple pie that i made myself; it was very good and we had plum pudding that was made between us which was very good.

Sunday 26th. Very calm and quiet.

Monday. Very calm and fine.

Tuesday. Very calm. Wet evening.

Wednesday 29th Dec. The Channel Pilot left the ship. The signal lights were lit about 8 Oclock in the evening; he went away at 10 Oclock. It seemed queer to one that knows nothing about sea life the way theay signal for boats to come to thc ship at night-time.

Thirsday 30th. Rather rough.

Friday 31st. We put into Plymouth Harbour to wait for a fair wind, which we had been in want of from the time of leaving London. When we got into the arbour there was some fishermen came with their boats wanting to tak the passengers ashore. When we were puting the ancour down one of their boats got fast with its mast into our main staysail roops and we where going about 5 Knots at the time so the boat sunk. There was three in the boat. One of theme got hold of the roops of our ship and got on bord; the other two were turned over into the water and one of them were drowned, a brother to the one that clung to our ship. I was standing looking over the side of the ship at the same time; it was a fearful sight to see them scrambling in the water.

Plymouth Arbour is a fine place; fine scienery all round. I went ashore Newyearsday. It seemed very queer with been on bord

ship so long, i ardley know how to use my legs ashore. I went
and got a good diner of a bit of fresh meat for a chainge and
it went down very good. I ardley knew how to sit at the table with
been use to the motion of the ship so much. I did not care much
about so much as i saw about but the arbour is spliended. I came
on bord in the afternoon and we sailed to sea about 7 Oclock
in the evening. It was lik begining another voyage.

Sunday 2nt Jan 1876. We had it rather rough at night also.

We sighted the lizerd lightHouse[4] on Monday morning. Clear
day, rather rough, so at that raite we have jus bee about three
weeks coming from the East India dock to the Chops of the
Channel — what we ought to of don in two or three days, so we
had a little knocking about. Some times we went back insted of
forred.

Thirsday 6th. Fine day, fair wind, going about 7 Knots an
Hour. We are on the outskirts of the Bay of biskey.[5] I thought
we should have to go through the bay, but onacount of the wind
we had to keep on the outskirts of the bay.
    I write a bit of song the sailors sing when theay are chainging
the tack and pulling som of the large roops. Theay stand still with
their hands on the roop and one man sings

> Once i had irish girl
> She was fat and lazey
> Then i had an English
> I keept her lik a ladie

Then theay all join in. Chorus Haul away Haul away Haul
away. Jow. That is for them all to give a regular pull every time
they finish the song.

---

[4]I.e., the lighthouse of Lizard Head, near the extreme southwestern tip of
England.

[5]I.e., the Bay of Biscay.

Friday. Very fine and good wind and good speed. Me and father started on a Harppoun for the boatswain; he is one of the officers of the ship.

Satuarday. Very little wind, very fine day.

Sunday [January 9th, 1876]. Fair wind, fine day. We had Church scervice in the saloon, the Captain reading the scervice. This was the first time since we been on bord we had a meat pie for dinner between us which we had to make ourselves. The cook bakes everything for us that we make.
We are on the coest of Portugal.

Monday. Fair wind, very fine day. Beautiful at night when the moon is shinig, something i often thought of when i was at Home.

Tuesday. Very fine and begining to get warm and we finished the Harpoun.

Wednesday. Good winds and very fine and we are geting the trade winds. I finished two little Hamers for the carppenter for making moddles of ships. I was barbering in the afternoon; i cut two men their air.
We had som fine fun about seven Oclock in the evening. The sailors were riging the dead Horse around the deck three or four times and singing all the time. It was an old cask dressed up like an Horse. Then theay pull it up to the yard harms then let it drop into the sea and then sing againe. The reason theay do this there was a month since we came from London and the Sailors got a months advance of wages before theay came on bord. Then theay recon theay have been working for dead Horse that month. I shall not forget riding the dead Horse; it was fine fun; the song theay were singing was this:

> Oh poor old man
> Your Horse will die
> If he does i'll tan his eyes
> Oh poor old man

Then theay all join in. Chorus: And i hope so, and i say so, Oh poor old man.

Thursday. Good wind and a very fine day. There was a fine sight around the ship at night; there was what theay call phospheric lights. It looks well when it is dark.

Friday. Good wind and very fine. Begining to get warm. About 12 Oclock at night we got into the tropics[6] so we are preparing for a roasting.

Satuarday. Good wind and very fine. I was cutting air to-day. Rather warm day.

Sunday [January 16th, 1876]. Very fine day, good wind. We saw som flying fish for the first time. We where at scervice in the morning in the salloon.

Monday. Very fine day. There was a flying fish caught for the first time by one of the passengers. Theay are much like a bird when theay are flying about the water.

Tuesday. Very fine, rather warm.

Wednesday. Very fine and warm.

Thirsday. Fine and very warm.

Friday. Very warm, nearly becalmed. Some of the passengers wer sleeping out on deck.

Satuarday. Very warm, in the morning heavey thunder and rain. It looked very much like a storm but it cleared up and was very fine after.

---

[6]I.e., the ship crossed the Tropic of Cancer.

Sunday [January 23rd, 1876]. Very warm, in the morning very heavey rain, thunder and lightning. We are in what theay call tropical storms; the rain is the only thing that denotes the winter this side of the line. We had scervice in the morning. I never saw so many fish about the ship as there was to-day.

Monday. Rather wet in the morning. Evening fine, rather warm.

Tuesday. Wet morning. We past a ship homewardbound from China. We signald her. She was going to London. Very fine ship she was; she looked well in the distance with all her sails set and the sun shining on her.
Heavey rain at night, it came down in sheets of water.

Wednesday. Beautiful day, rather warm, very little wind. We are about 41 mills from the line.

Thirsday Januarey 27th 1876. We wherc on the line to-day about 11 Oclock.[7] It is a very fine day, rather warm. We saw som very large fish; theay where like walles but theay were what theay call Gramphuses. Theay were white.

Friday. Very warm, a little more wind than we have had. We have had it very quiet.

Satuarday. Heavey fall of rain this morning then it cleared up and was very warm and a very good wind. The sea is a little rougher than it as been this last week or two.

Sunday [January 30th, 1876]. Very fine, rather warm, good wind. I was [at] scervice in the morning, we only have scervice in the mornings.

---

[7]Griffiths makes no mention of a traditional "crossing the Line" ceremony. Perhaps Shaw Savill or the master forbade it on the ground of its potential abuses.

Monday. Fine day and good wind. I had a heavey wash this morning. I washed three blankets and shirts and two sheets and white jacket; i had them in a large bath and danced on them with my bare feet. We had rain water what we had catched with the heavey rains. This is Scotch fashion of wasshing.

I had two blankets and two sheets given to me by a young fellow, a meddical student. He was going out to Newzealand but he rewed. When we where in the Channel theay put him ashore at the Isle of white. He intended going there on plesseure and to Australia and America hunting princible and he wanted me to go with him and pay my expences all over and 40 pounds when i came home with him. He gave me his photo just before he went of the ship.

Tuesday. Very fine and good breeze. I got rather sun burnt the other day. One dose not feel it when the sun is burning him because of the breeze that is blowing; then when the sun as gon down you feel it very sharp. It would be rosting if it was not for the breeze; the sun is direct over our heads.

Wednesday. Fine day, rather warm, good breeze. We had one of the sails blown to pieces this morning.

Thirsday. Very fine and warm with rather a light breeze. There as a heavey squall through the night. In the evening there was one of the most beautiful sun sets ever i saw; the sun set in the trophics are beautiful.

Friday. Very fine day, light breeze. Evening some very heavey squalls and heavey rains.

Satuarday. Very fine and rather warm. We are not more than about 100 milles of the Chost of Brazils; i never thought that we should run so close to America.

Sunday [February 6th, 1876]. Very fine and very warm. We were all at scervice this morning.

Monday. Very warm. It came on very wet in the evening; it rained to middle night.

Tuesday. Very fine and rather warm. There is very little wind and that makes it much warmer.

Wednesday. Very warm. The sea is like one sheet of glass. We are juist about becalmed.

Thirsday. Very fine, very little wind, very near becalmed.

Friday. Very fine and rather warm and we have a little more wind.

Satuarday. Very dul day. Little rain and a little more wind.

Sunday [February 13th, 1876]. Very dull and wet day. We were at scervice in the morning. It is geting a bit colder now.

Monday. Heavey rain in the morning; fine day after and a good breeze.

Tuesday. Very wet day, good breeze, sea rather rougher than it as been this good while.

Wednesday. A bit finer, the wind and sea as gon down. There was an Albortross caught this morning by one of the passengers. It is a fine bird; it is about as large as a swan. It messers 10 feet 2 in. from tip to tip of the wings.

Thirsday. Very fine and a good breeze.

Friday. Very fine day, the sea is as smooth as glass. Becalmed. There was another fine Albortross caught this morning and some Cap hens, by some of the passengers. The Cape hens mesure from 6 to 7 feet tip to tip of wing.

Satuarday. Fine day, good breeze and rather cold. We feel the cold very much after aving it so warm.

Sunday [February 20th, 1876]. Very rough day, very heavey wind blowing. We where at scervice this morning and in the middle of the scervice the Captain had to go away; one of the staysails had blown away, the wire rope had broken. So one of the passengers took his place. The sea as a very stormey appearance. It cleared up a little better at night. We are on what theay call the rough forties, that is the latitude.

Monday. Very foggie morning, the sea as gon down a great deal since yesterday, it is rather cold. Evening and night the sea rose up very much.

Tuesday. Wether a little better, very good breeze.

Wednesday. Wether fine, rather cold, good breeze. We are what theay [call] runing the Easter down.[8]

Thirsday. Fine day, cold, rather less wind.

Friday. Fine day, good breeze, rather cold.

Satuarday. Fine day, wind gon down a great deal. It causes a great deal of roling when the wind goes down because the wind leaves a dead swell in the sea. There was some wails seen to-day but i was bellow so i never saw them. There was a good breeze got up at night.

Sunday [February 27th, 1876]. Wett morning, ardley aney wind. We had scervice in the morning.

---

[8]"Running the Easting Down" — a phrase denoting the route taken by sailing ships running east in the Southern latitudes.

Monday. Fine day, good breeze, rather cold. Heavey sea running.

Tuesday. Fine day, not quite so cold. Wind, very little. At night the wind rose again; there was a strong breeze; one of the sails carried away.

Wednesday. Fine day, good breeze.

Thirsday. Whet. Dirty cold. A very strong wind and a high sea runing.

Friday. Very wet and cold day, not quite as much wind.

Satuarday. Not quite so wet but very fogie and rather cold. Very little wind.

Sunday [March 5th, 1876]. Fine day, quite a chaing from the last few days, a nice breeze springing up. We had scervice in the morning.

Monday. Dull day and rather cold. Hed winds. We have not been able to get an altitude this last few days because there was no sun.

There was one or two birds shot by some of the passengers on the poope called mothers carless chickings or Stormie pedrills.[9] Theay are very small birds and there is a great deal of suppperstition attached to them. The sailors and officers belive that there is a great deal of bad luck whe there is aney of them killed of the ship. I saw one of the Midshipmen[10] catch one of them and one of the officers saw him; he took it of him and let it go. Theay

----

[9]The stormy petrel, commonly called "Mother Carey's chickens."

[10]"Midshipmen" is primarily a naval term. Griffiths must be referring to one of *Euterpe*'s apprentices, of which she carried four on this voyage. One of these, Oswald Letts, aged 16, fell from aloft on July 24th and died of his injuries on August 1st, 1876.

reckon that is the cause of our bad wether just now through catching those birds.

Tuesday. Cold day and very little wind. There was a fine Albortross caught about 10 Oclock at night, the first that have been caught at night-time. We have two of their feet for tobaco pouches; theay make fine pouches. There is fine pipe stems to be got out of their wings. I have got a wing and a foot.

Steerage passengers study their ship's progress in this old Victorian woodcut.
SOURCE: KARL KORTUM, NATIONAL MARITIME MUSEUM, SAN FRANCISCO

Wednesday. Fine day. We are at a standstill; there is no wind. There was two other fine Albortross caught to-day. It is something singlure to be at a standstill in those latitudes by all accounts. I saw some very large wails this evening. Theay made fearful noise, you could hear them a long way off when theay did blow.

Thirsday. Fine morning, rather cold.

Friday. Cold damp day, good breeze. Very strong wind through the night; theay had to take a deal of sail of her.

Satuarday. Strong breeze, heavey sea runing. Tons of water comin over the forecastle. One of the sailors was very near washed of the jibboom. He clung olt of the roops as the sea came over him and when he came up he was turned upside down. Them that saw him go thought sure he was dun for. He was soon allright again.

Sunday [March 12th, 1876]. Very fine day, very little wind. In the morning we had scervice. Evening, a very strong breeze came on.

Monday. Fine day, rather cold, good breeze. At night it came on very wield; it took one all is time to keep in is bunk. There was some rolled out of bed, infact everything was turned upside down by the morning.

Tuesday. Heavey sea runing, very strong breez and rather cold.

Wednesday. Fine day, rather cold, breeze falling off. A good breeze sprung up again at night.

Thirsday. Fine day, rather cold, good breeze. Heavey sea runing, tons of water coming over her deck. One of the sheets broke away in the evening. There was quite a gail during the night; the wind was making a fearful whistling noise all night and the ship was going very fast.

Friday. Fine day, very cold, good breeze, heavey sea runing.

Satuarday. Fine morning, very cold, good breeze, wind rather getting ahead of us. At night very rough; tons of water coming over her fore and aft. When it is rough like this it makes it very bad for us to go to the gallie with our hookpots for tea or coffee or aney thing to bake. We often get a good ducking with the sea coming over the side; it is laughable when there is no one urt.

Sunday [March 19th, 1876]. Very cold, dull day. Good breeze and a heavey sea runing.

Monday. Fine day, not so rough. Rather a high wind.

Tuesday. Fine day, not quit so cold. Fair wind but very little of it.

Wednesday. Very fine day, like sumer in England. It is quite a treet after aving such bad wether. We have very little wind. We caught two mollie Auks[11] to-day.

Thirsday. Very cold, fair wind, rather wet. Very Strong breeze through the night.

Friday. Very cold, but fine day and good breeze.

Satuarday. Fine, not quite so cold and good breeze. We are in *Australian waters*. It came on very rough and squallie through the night.

Sunday [March 26th, 1876]. Clear, fine day, rather cold. Very strong breeze, very heavey sea runing. The waves theay are like mountains, coming over her in tons. We had a heavey hower of aille stones this morning; this is the roughest sea i have seen yet.
We had no scervice this morning; the captain was out all night and all day so you may gues it was very rough.

Monday. Fine, clear day, rather cold. Heavey sea runing, good breeze, not quite so rough as yesterday. There was heavey squalls of ailstons during the day. At night it came on very bad.

---

[11]Mollyhawks or mallemucks.

Tuesday. Wet, cold, dirty day. Strong breeze. Very heavey sea runing, tons of water coming over her right and left. One canot get on deck but very little when it is lik this. If on dose come on deck he is apt to get washed from one side to the other. Heavey squalls of ailstons at night.

Wednesday. Very cold, dul day. Not so rough as it have been. At night it came in fearfule wield.

Thirsday. Fearfule rough, a living gail. Sea like mountains and the wind is wistling through the rigging. Three of the sails blown away to ribbons. It is quite daingerous to go on deck. The sailors is having a rough time of it, the sea coming over all roads in tons. One of the officers got lamed on deck. Very rough through the night.

Friday. Very rough, heavey sea runing, not quite so bad as yesterday. I went on deck this morning to have a look round. It was a queer sight to see the sails hanging about her all in ribbons; it showd that [we?] had a rough time of it. At night the wind died away. The Captain said that he never saw such a gail this four years.[12]

Satuarday, April 1st. Fine day, rather cold, very little wind. Sea nearley calm. One can ardley believe that the sea could go down so sudden with been so rough the days before. Me and father was at work to-day doing some repairs for the ship. She had a lot of things broken with the gail.

Sunday [April 2nd, 1876]. Very fine day, nice breeze. It is quite a treat after aving it so rough.

Monday. Fine day, good breeze. Rather a heavey sea runing. Rather squallie through the night with ailstons.

---

[12]This was Captain Phillips's fourth voyage in *Euterpe.*

Tuesday. Fine day, good breeze.

Wednesday. Very dul day; head wind. Evening it came in very fogie; theay were blowing the fog orn till about 8 Oclock. Then it came on thundering and lightning very heavey till all the sea was in one elumination for about an hour or two. Then we had a chaing of wind and the fog cleard away and we had it very rough the night.

Thirsday. Very fine day, good breeze, heavey sea runing and very fine night.

Friday. Very fine day, clear sky all round and good breeze. Fine night.

Satuarday. Very fine day, good breeze. We are very near our destination; it seems queer to be counting days instead of months. We past the *snairs this evening.*[13] Theay are a lot of rocks in the sea; theay look like mountains and islands. We where very near when we were pasing them. Every bodie seemed to rejoice to see something like land before them as we have onley seen two ships since we left Plymouth. It was quite a treete to see those *rocks.*

Sunday [April 9th, 1876]. Very dul day, fair breeze.

Monday. Very fine, rather cold. To-day we had the first sight of Newzealand. It looks very queer, all mountains and ills and snow on the top of them. It is the part called Otago. It causes a sensation all over the ship to see land. The sailors are geting the chains and ancours ready to land. [sic]

Tuesday. Very fine day, not so cold as yesterday. We are very close to land. It is beautiful scienery all round the sea shore, all woods and forests and in the distance we can see the Cichoria

---

[13]The Snares are a cluster of rocky islands and islets below the southern end of South Island, New Zealand.

mountains[14] all covered with perpetual snow. It looks beautiful with the sun shining on them. I like the look of the countrey very much by what i can see of it from the ship. We got towed with a screw boat into arbour — it is a fine arbour, something lik Plymouth Arbour.

We dropt Ancour at 3 Oclock this Afternoon. Everything seems very quiet about here and it is nice and warm so this is the end of one journey. John Griffiths Landed in Portlyttlton[15] Tuesday April 11th, 1876.

Me and father left the ship Euterpe with all our luggage in a small boat to-day, Wednesday April 12th, and went on bord the screw boat called the Taupo. We sailed out of arbour about 5 Oclock this evening. We had no knives, forks & plates to find; every thing found on bord and a steward to wait on us — it is nothing like the Euterpe. She is a fine large screw ship. Ther is a lot of passengers of bord; theay come on bord here just like theay do to go to Middlesbro or Stockton at home.[16] We had a comfortable night.

Thirsday. Fine morning. We arived at Wellington at 9 Oclock this morning. We went ashore for a few hours wile theay dischaged her. It is a fine little town, all wooden buildings, and there is a good bit of shiping don here; there is som very large vessels in the arbour. Wile we were in town we saw several natives here, men, wimen & children. The moest of the men are tattooed in the face; theay look very curious people.

We left here about 2 Oclock. We are the onley ones left of the Euterpe lot. There [are] plenty of straing passengers on bord. We are going it rather rough. We are in Cooks straights.[17] After

---

[14]Griffiths apparently refers to the Southern Alps.

[15]I.e., Port Lyttelton near Christchurch.

[16]Griffiths refers to Middlesbrough and Stockton-on-Tees in the north of England. Apparently he had lived not far away.

[17]I.e., Cook Strait.

Picton, 1872

COURTESY OF AVON FINE PRINTS LTD., CHRISTCHURCH, N.Z.

we got out of the straights we went through a very narow Place
called the french path, 20 milles long from the mouth of it up
to a place called Picton. There was on of the most curious things
appned. A star fell into the water; it seemed like a slag ball and
it opened like a bell; it seemed to drop into the water in front
of us. There were severel old colinests on bord said theay never
saw aney thing like it afore in their lives. This water twists and
turns like an horse shoe; it is all curves. Aneyone would wonder
how theay fetch such larg vessels up. One could nearley jump
ashore at times, it is that narrow, but very deep and as full of
fish as evere it can stick, and we saw som very large porposes here.
I should think it is one of the queerest passeges in Newzealand.
We left Picton about middle night for Nelson.[18]

Friday. Very fine and warm. We arived in Nelson about 10
Oclock this morning. It is a fine place. We have to transship here
for Hockiticika.[19] As it apned to be Good Friday it was a general
Holiday so we had to sleep here one night. We had to pay one
shilling for each meal and a shilling for a bed. We had fresh meat
every meal, the same on bord the steamers here all round the costs.

Satuarday. Fine, very warm day just like England in the middle of sumer. It is the fall of the year here. We had the chance
of work here in a week or twos time if we would stop. We sailed
out of Nelson at 3 Oclock this afternoon in a steam boat called
Kennedy. We had a queer night of it; she is not such a fine boat
as the Taupo. We arived in Westport at 11 Oclock.[20]

Sunday morning [April 16th, 1876]. It is a fine morning and
rather warm. We went ashore. It is not such a fine place as Nelson
nor so large. It is a little flatter and all forest; there is more wood
cuting and clearing of than aney thing else. We went to church

---

[18]Picton and Nelson are towns on the north coast of South Island, N.Z.

[19]Hokitika is a town on the west coast of South Island.

[20]Westport is on the west coast of South Island.

in the evening for the first time in the colinies. The sermon was took from the 24 chapter of Luke. It is a very nice little church but very few people there. It is all wood building here.

Monday. Wet, raining all day. I saw a couple of canoes on the river with maories[21] in them. Theay were bringing garden produce into town; there was men, wimen and children in the canoes.

Tuesday. Very wet, raining all day.

Wednesday. Quite a chainge, very fine, quite warm. We leave here at 6 Oclock this evening. We have been here four days. The reason we stop here so long is because the rivers are all flooded and we could not get into the other ports.

Thirsday. We arrived at Hoktika at 8 Oclock this morning. It is very wet here, raining all the time. We went ashore. It is a large place and every thing seems very slack, ardley aney thing doing.

Friday. Very wet. We find we canot get aney thing to do here so we are going away again. Father he is going to Greaymouth[22] and i am going to Nelson with the same boat, but we are shour bound here for a few days on account of the bad wether and floods with the heavey rain that as fallen.

Satuarday. Not quite so much rain. I was up to the Canarie Gold diggings, theay are about four mils of Hockitika. Every thing seemed deserted, nothing going on there, just a small town ship there and very quiet.

Sunday [April 23rd, 1876]. Fine morning. We left here at 8 Oclock this morning for Greaymouth. We arived here at 11 Oclock this morning; it is very fine here. We went ashore around. Things

---

[21] I.e., Maoris, the native people of New Zealand.

[22] Greymouth is on the west coast of South Island, above Hokitika.

look a little better than Hockitika and by all acounts mor work here.

We went a little way out into the countrey and we came across a maorie man and wooman and theay began to try to talk to us. Theay could onley talk a word or two of English, then theay broke into their own language. We thought there was something the matter because there was a lot of people going that way and the maorie was saying "tipo" fell over and making motions. And when we got along a bit we came to where a man and horse had fell over a presipes. Theay were pulling the horse up with rops. The maories came up and theay were saying one tipo to much beer one tip to little. Theay ment one devil had to much beer the other too little.

We went to church in the evening, it was a very nice place all built of wood.

Monday. Fine morning. The river here divids Nelson province and Westland. There is a small place called Cobton on the other side of the water which is in the province of Nelson. There is a great maney people leaving here fore the Palmer diggings in Austrilia. There is a lot of China men her, more than i have saw aney were yet. Father got work here. He as to go to a Place called Riefton to work, about 54 miles inland. He as to go with a coach; is wages is £4 per week for the first month, then he will be roase. He will comence work begining of May.

Tuesday. Dul damp day and great deal of rain. Cleard up again at night.

Wednesday. Wet morning. I left here alone with the same boat at 11 Oclock this morning for Nelson. Arived at Westport at 8 Oclock. We stopet here all night.

Thirsday. Fine morning. We leave here at 10 Oclock this morning.

Friday. We arived Nelson 7 Oclock this morning. It is very fine here and rather warm.

Satuarday. Very quiete here, it puts me in mind of Saltburn or Redcar.[23] I am staing in a hotel here called the Albion. He is a darkie named McKenzie. [sic] It is a very comfortable place. I have a bed room to myself in the front of the House. I have to go out side to the stairs from the back of the House. It is quite a treat to me for to be in a House after Knocking about so much on bord vessels, it is the first time for me to have a rest since i left home. I got plentey of good tucker; that is what theay call the food here.

Sunday [April 30th, 1876]. Very wet day, raining nearley all day.

Monday. Very wet day. Work seams very scarce here.

Tuesday. Very fine and warm.

Wednesday. It is the first day of the races. Theay are held about four miles of here.

Thirsday. Fine day, we had a heavey shour of rain. This is a race day too. There is two days of races here. There is not so much talk and fuss here as there is at home.

[Friday, Saturday, Sunday]. We had fine wether the remainder of the week.

Monday, May 8th, 1876. I got a start work here. I was just going to pack up my swag and go to a place called Collingwood[24] when i was asked if i would start work labouring with the brother-in-law of the manneger at 8 shillings per day till something better turns up.
So i started work. I thought it would be better than tramping about this winter as people seams to dread the winter about this countrey. If i had gon to Collingwood i should of gon on the gold

---

[23]Saltburn and Redcar are towns on the North Sea coast of Yorkshire in England.
[24]The town is near Cape Farewell at the northern tip of South Island.

diggings and chanced my luck. Joinering is as good a trade out here as aney trade i know of. Theay are all wooden buildings. There their wages is from [blotted out] to [blotted out] shillings per day. I gained 16 pounds in weight since i left home to the time i came to Nelson. So this is the end of my travels for a wile.

John Griffiths, Nelson, 1876

VI.

THE VOYAGE OF 1879:
GEORGE LISTER
AND THE BROTHERS OWEN

1879: A MOMENT IN TIME

By 1879, London was the looking glass of the world. The great city reflected the brilliant noon of England's power and glory. Much of this is apparent in the following pages, as *Euterpe* is delayed in sailing, giving her passengers several days to wander about the imperial capital.

What did the city look like? Like any major metropolis, it assumed the look of its people. On the jostling thoroughfares of morning, bummarees and buskers swarmed about, singing, swearing, peddling their wares. At night, hansom cabs clip-clopped down the Mall, lit by the flare of gas lamps. Broadsides bannered the war news from Britain's latest colonial conflicts — against the Afghans at the Khyber Pass and the Zulus of South Africa. In the popular prints, *Vanity Fair, The Times,* and the "penny dreadfuls" (analogous to modern tabloids) each claimed an audience.

For the poor of Bluegate Fields and other urban slums, life might be harsh; for the middle class in the newest pubs, thick amidst brass, glass and warm brown ale, life was good and getting better. Recruiting sergeants strolled along in pillbox caps and Norfolk jackets, their latest charges in tow. Gentlemen tipped their hats to ladies, and servant girls on "'alf-holiday" exchanged coy looks with "other ranks." Stevedores sweated in the East End, and a blind man in a ragged coat played his violin for pennies in the Strand. Horse-drawn fire companies clattered toward the nearest blaze, white horses snorting, steam swirling, men shouting and bell rattling away.

The sun never set on the city's influence. In the august chambers of the Bank of England in Threadneedle Street, men in somber black suits guided the fates of nations as well as of private fortunes. In the houses of Lords and Commons, small cliques determined the political destinies of millions—white, black, yellow, brown—around the globe.

One did not gain admittance to these places on the basis of wealth alone. One had to be "of the right sort." The same applied to gaining a commission in the Army or Navy, entering the church, the law, and certain other professions. There were gentlemen's rules, gentlemen's agreements, and gentlemen's very private clubs.

Although the system certainly had its limitations, it was not insensible to change and progress. For the vast majority of Englishmen, it worked perfectly well. Decisions were made and Government run on the basis of personal acquaintance (always within one's class, of course). "A nod could be made to tell," in Winston Churchill's nostalgic phrase.

But this society was not for all. Certain men and women found it too restrictive, even stifling. These were generally people of talent and industry who belonged to the lower classes. For them, the colonies beckoned. Leave the farm or the cobbler's shop behind, if you would muster the courage: take yourself to London, there to obtain a passage "out east"—to Australia, perhaps, or distant New Zealand.

Once plunked down safe and sound in Sydney, Melbourne, Wellington or Christchurch, the class distinctions didn't seem to matter so much. There was plenty of opportunity for all. And so the emigration tide continued to grow.

England wasn't the world, of course (it only seemed so to some of the men in those august chambers). What else was going on in 1879?

Across the Atlantic, Rutherford Birchard Hayes was the 19th President of the United States. Once in office, he ended Reconstruction in the South by withdrawing Federal troops, and began to clean up some of the scandals left behind by the Grant Administration. The very picture of Victorian rectitude in his top hat and long frock coat, the bearded Hayes seemed to restore the people's confidence. American business boomed along, with tycoons like William Henry Vanderbilt and John D. Rockefeller leading the pack. Vast new mansions began to rise along Fifth Avenue in New York, symbolizing the new prosperity. Chicago and San Francisco built their mansions, too. A new political party, the Greenbacks, appeared. Farmers were organizing in the National Grange, and labor unions began to gather strength. The marvelous new inventions continued to come: in New Jersey, a man named Thomas Edison patented an improved electric light. Immigrants poured into New York's slums from Europe, and there was talk of building some sort of monument in the harbor to the oncoming millions.

In the West, news of a gold strike in the Arizona desert spread fast; opportunists of every stripe were soon heading for sun-bleached towns like Bisbee, Douglas, Tombstone. Over in the New Mexico Territory, the "Lincoln County War" between various ranchers and outlaw elements had burned out — but lawless men were still rustling cattle and killing, among them a 19-year-old gunman named Henry McCarty, alias William Bonney, alias "Billy, the Kid."

In Europe, the Russo-Turkish War had ended the previous year. Russia's hard-won victory had not been welcomed by other powers; Germany and Austria-Hungary signed a pact of alliance in 1879, and together were subsequently termed the Central Powers. It was the first in the web of alliances that would lead to the world catastrophe of 1914-18.

In South America the War of the Pacific broke out, the main antagonists being Chile and Peru. The war saw several naval actions testing the new turret ironclads and ship-launched torpedoes. The British observed with particular interest, as combatants on both sides ordered ships from Laird's of Birkenhead and other yards in Britain. The war at length ended with Chile's extension to the north, at the expense of Bolivia and Peru.

In Afghanistan, England's Lord Roberts marched on Kabul. The Second Afghan War was a struggle fought as much against terrain as the natives, but led to a stabilization of India's Northwest Frontier. In South Africa, England's Lord Chelmsford had less success against the Zulus. A Zulu *impi* (army) overran two battalions of the 24th Foot in the shadow of a mountain called Isandhlwana; some 900 redcoats and 470 native auxiliaries died to a man. The Zulus were superb fighters; it would require reinforcements plus plenty of Gatling guns and breech-loading artillery before their spears were downed.

But all these things were of distant concern. To the English, Scottish, Welsh, Irish and European emigrants who gathered in London to board a ship named *Euterpe*, all that mattered was that they were bound for the promised land of New Zealand.

GEORGE LISTER, THE BROTHERS OWEN, AND THE *EUTERPE*

Euterpe was a globe-trotting veteran now, and this was her seventh trip around the world for Shaw Savill. She began by easing out of East India Dock, London, on August 2nd. Captain Thomas Phillips was again in command.

In those days, rivers teeming with traffic were not the safest of places for a ship to loiter. Scarcely was *Euterpe* out in the Thames, riding at anchor, than a steamer plowed into her starboard bow, driving her astern and into a third vessel.

Once everyone calmed down, the damage assessment included a very large hole in *Euterpe*'s bow above the waterline. Back she went into East India Dock for eight days of repairs. (It should have been seven, but the day following the accident was Bank Holiday—and nary a dockyard worker to be had.)

This collision, it might be noted, was neither the first nor the last for *Euterpe*. In 1864 a Spanish brig brushed her off the coast of Wales, and her jibboom carried away. That and other damage caused her to limp back to Anglesey, where the magistrates clapped her mutinous crew into Beaumaris Gaol.

In years to come, *Euterpe* seemed to develop a talent for becoming the hitter instead of the hittee, and she would waltz with such unwilling partners as the steamer *Canadian* in the Clyde, and the barkentine *Sir John Franklin* at Newcastle, New South Wales.

Later in her career, the *Euterpe* collided with the barkentine *Sir John Franklin* in Australia. This portrait of the English barkentine *Waterwitch* (1871) shows the rig. Barkentines were more economical to operate than full-rigged ships, having square sails only on the foremast.

SOURCE: NATIONAL MARITIME MUSEUM, LONDON, U.K.

In fairness to the skippers of the time, a ship on the move is a difficult thing to stop. This was even more true for sailing ships: clearly, one could not reverse engines; about all that *could* be done quickly was to put the helm hard over and pray.

As if this tete-a-tete in the Thames was not frightening enough, once *Euterpe* got under way (August 12th) and commenced knocking about in the Channel (August 13th), she nearly had a second smash. As a diary details, a likely fatal encounter with the ship *Hurunui* was averted only when the latter sheered off at the last second—with curses and catcalls from *Euterpe's* crew following.

Poor *Euterpe* went on knocking about for quite a while, being blown back from South Foreland to North Foreland, and later from the Atlantic to the Lizard. This voyage was to be one of her most galling for Captain Phillips. Contrary winds and hazardous sea conditions reduced *Euterpe* to a crawling pace, and she finished up at Lyttelton after 144 days at sea (125 land to land).

When the ship made port on Christmas Eve, after a Jonah voyage of nearly five months, among the passengers crowding her decks was one George J. Lister, late of Broughton, Cumberlandshire. Mr. Lister committed to paper the most detailed account we have concerning a voyage of *Euterpe*. We publish most of it here. As with the Griffiths diary, every effort has been made to retain its flavor. The editor added some punctuation and paragraphed more, to improve clarity. Wording has not been touched, however. The only parts of the diary not included are those devoted to lengthy lists of passengers competing in various contests, the amounts of their prizes, etc. In a few places, it was necessary to correct spelling—e.g., Mr. Lister's persistence in spelling "who" as "how." Otherwise, spelling has been left as in the original diary.

Also aboard was a family named Owen—a mother and four sons. Poor Mrs. Owen never had time to gain her sea legs—she took a tumble in a gale and broke one of them. Her sons, aged 9 to 16, tended her as *Euterpe* lurched and rammed through the seas to their new home. Many years later, two of these sons— Alexander and Ernest—recalled the voyage in correspondence, which we publish towards the end of this chapter. The youngest Owen, Llewellyn, had a bit of the Welsh bard in him: he grew up to become a composer, and later wrote a piece for piano, "The Euterpe Waltz." We print its cover as a *finis* to Part One—and to the voyage of 1879.

"A DIARY KEPT BY GEORGE J. LISTER ON HIS PASSAGE FROM ENGLAND TO NEW ZEALAND IN THE YEAR 1879"

To Mr. J. B. Lister
Broughton

I left Brigham Station on Tuesday 29th day of July 1879 by the 7 Oclock P.M. Train, and arrived in Carlisle about 9 Oclock. We went to Aunts and had a look through Carlisle untill train time, which left at 12.40 and arrived at Easton Square Station, London at 8.40 A.M. J. Archer and I left our luggage in the office and went to Gowerstreet Station and took the train to Aldersgate but we should have taken it to Aldsgate. So we had a good way to walk to Leadenhall Street to Shaw & Savills office.

They recommended us to stay at 47 Whitechapel St. We stayed two nights. On Wednesday afternoon the day we arrived we got a few things we needed and took a Cab to take our luggage to the East India Docks and left them in the warehouse, as none had to be taken on Ship untill Friday. We had to pay Docks dues which was one shilling per Box and six pence per parcel. It don't matter the size of Boxes, all pays alike.

The men in the warehouse puts the luggage on Board for all. But you must be on the ship to tell them where you want the boxes put or they will put them all in the holds. As when they started to put ours on, I went down the fore hatch to see that those were not put down we wanted on the voyage, while Archer was to stay on deck to see that the Boxes came on ship all right. But I had only got one of mine down when the luggage had all come on board. I went up but it was a while before I found Archer; he had never watched at all and did not know whether they had come on the ship or not. So we went to the Warehouse but they were not there. And Archer was in a sad way when he thought he had lost both of his. About a week after I went down the Second class hold and found mine and one of Archers but his other he did not get for three weeks aftcr, when I went again to look for it.

We did not see much of London as it was raining most time of the three days we were in. We went on Board *the ship Euterpe* about 7 Oclock Friday evening the *first of August* and [were] taken to the entrance of the dock by the steam tug Napolean [sic], where she lay untill one Oclock A.M. Saturday, when she was tuged down the river to Gravesend and stayed there for the Government inspector. He came and went away so we moored there for the night waiting for the doctor. We all enjoyed ourselves very much untill nine Oclock when some went to bed.

But singing and playing was going on in our compartment when she was run into by a large Steam Ship named Talford and cut her cable from the Buoy and sent us a-drift. It run into the fore-end on the Starboard side, and sent the hinder-end into another vessel which was moored close bye named Hahneman. So both ends of the vessel we were on was smashed. We that were below could not tell what was to do as she seemed to be full of Smoke. We got on deck as sharp as we could and that was not very sharp as one pulled another back while trying to get up first. When we got on deck the watchman was laying and severely hurt and another of the sailors had his head cut for she was run into where they were laying. There was great confusion on the ship as they thought she was sinking and we were up to the knees in water on deck; some run up the masts. [sic] Here's a verse which appeared in the papers. —

> Oh Panic was then rife on deck,
> And folks rushed too and fro,
> And Oaths and prayers and Dolby Cans
> Were strangly mixed with woe.

But steam tugs and boats soon came all round, and the men saw the hole was above water, although it was very large. But they were not long in getting her moored again. The Steamer that struck us went ashore with the force of the blow and had to waite to the next tide to get off.

We lay at Buoy untill Sunday. We had several ministers on board speaking untill 11 Oclock when she was taken back to the docks to get repairs. At night, it being Sunday, I and another in the same mess went to the Methodist Free church in Commercial road. After we came back there was service on board.

On Monday 4th inst. was Bank Holiday and more shops were closed than on a Sunday and the workmen would not start with the ship. Tuesday 5th they commenced and worked nearly night and day.

There were two Stowaways on board; they turned out after the collision; they were taken to-day and searched and any thing they had was taken from them. They were then taken to court to be tried; they were about 18 and 19 years of age. Anyone is allowed to come on board. And there as been many things missing. So some one stayes to look after things while others are away.

There was a meeting called, they said for our wellfare and a petition sent to Shaw & Savill against our allowance and the doctor. So we have got a fresh Doctor. At nights the mates and Police of the Docks came below to put [out] our lights at nine Oclock, as no lights were allowed in the Docks after that hour. But one night a disturbance took place, and after that they were kept burning all night. The ships Company finds lights to burn all night. So there was no use for the candles we bought.

The East India Docks are walled all round and four doors into them, and a police Stationed at each door. And whatever is carried in or out they look at it and after six Oclock the doors are fastened and we have to tell them the name of the Ship we are going too.

We have plenty of time to look about a part of London. I have been in St. Pauls twice, once at service. It is a grand place; there are fine Monuments in it of nearly all the great men who have distinguished themselves at war.

And I was through the Tower of London; it is a large dismal place. And in the Yard there are large Cannons of all kinds, and the soldiers were going through their drill. And in the rooms the sides are all covered with swords, Guns, and Armour that have been used and worn at different ages and in different lands, and those that have been taken at war by the British, and those presented to them. The finest large Gun in the world is there. It was taken from Malta by the Egyptians, and from them by the French, and taken from the French by the British at Sea. There are all the Kings and Queens with their armour on, and on Horse Back. And the blocks, and axes, where the Kings, and others who have been beheaded, have had there heads cut off with, also the masks the executioners wore. In the places where the prisoners were kept, there are many names and different figures cut out on the walls. There is a room where the crowns and jewels are kept; they are splendid.

I was through the British Museum; a very large one it is. Also the National Gallery, in Trafalgar Square. It is a fine Square; there are two large fountains with ponds, and in the Gallery there are some very fine pictures. I and another went to the houses of Parliament, got papers to go through, and through the house of Lords and the Queen's chamber; they are fine places, and very large buildings. Also through the West Minister Abbey as it is close bye; it is a grand place for Architecture and ancient Monuments. We took the boat from West Minister to the Docks about seven miles. But it was very slow having so many calls; it took us about two hours.

On Sunday 10th three of us went to Mr. Spurgeon's Tabernacle. We took the boat to London Bridge six miles and then had a mile to walk. We got there about 10.30 A.M. We had to waite untill eleven Oclock. About the doors outside was crowded, and when we got inside we scarce could get a seat. A good many had to stand; there was the most people gathered together in a place I ever saw. He took for his text Mathew 13ch. 12ve. and read and commented on the same chapter. When we came out we walked to the Metropolitan Station; we then took the tram to the docks which was sooner and not half the price as the Boat. We had different people on board preaching in the evening. Some of the Salvation army came a few times. They have a fine place of worship in Whitechapel St.

On *Monday 11th* there was notice put up that all passengers of the *Euterpe had to be on board* that night.

On Tuesday 12th they got the ship all right and we were taken out of dock by the steam tug Renown and taken to Gravesend, where we stayed awhile for the inspector, and gave up part of our Tickets. We then were tuged down the river. It is a beautiful country on both sides of the Thames.

Wednesday 13th. Sighted South-Foreland and Dover.

Thursday 14th. The Pilot left us, and the Tug, but we got another Pilot on the same day, and a few of us started to be sick.

On Friday 15th it was very fine but in the evening it came on very rough.

Saturday 16th. It came a gale.

Sunday 17th. The Sea was awful; the waves comming over the ship, and all very bad with sickness and we sighted North Foreland.[1]

Monday 18th. The sea was calm but wind against us, so we only make tacks across the channel.

Tuesday 19th. The sea very rough and sickness no better. The Mate started to give out the rashings.[2] You can see on their papers what they are, but everything is the poorest. And the Cooks so greedy that we cannot get a drop of warm fresh water to mix anything we want. So it is very little that we eat.

Wednesday 20th. The sea very rough, wind against us, or head wind.

About five Oclock in the evening we had a very narrow escape of a collision with a sailling vessal named Hurunui, one of the New Zealand Shipping Company's ships.[3] She had two or three

---

[1]North Foreland is some 15 miles north of South Foreland, sighted on the 13th. This meant the gale had blown the ship back some distance.

[2]I.e., the rations. Apparently the passengers had used up whatever food they had brought along by this date.

hundred emigrants on board for New Zealand from Plymouth. The rough wether had kept her in the channel. She doubled twice in front of us, and was then comming straight on our broad side. The sails were set against our ship and brought her to a stand still[4] but the other was comming broad side, in front of us. The Pilot said we could not get clear of her, and both ships would be in danger of going down. All were called on deck, some had cork belts tied on, some their Dolby water Cans, but when she

Here is a typical British windjammer crew of the late Victorian period. This lot is on board the *Isle of Arran* in San Diego in 1894. We have no photographs of any crew of the *Euterpe,* but in their dress and general appearance, they must have looked much the same. Note the visiting lady and children on the ladder.

MACMULLEN COLLECTION

---

[3]The *Hurunui* had been launched in 1875, and was of nearly identical size with the *Euterpe.* She later collided with and sank the *Waitara* of her own line in the Channel (June 22nd, 1883). She eventually passed into Russian hands under the name *Hermes,* and was reported afloat as late as 1921.

[4]I.e., the *Euterpe's* sails were set aback.

98

was a few Yards off a breeze took her off. Her sails touched the sails of our ship. Her decks were crowded with passengers, but not a cheer was given, as to all other ships that passed, but the Pilot and sailors on our ship told them to throw their Captain overboard.

Thursday 21st. The Pilot left us by a steam boat. We sighted Dungeness, and Beachy Head, and Isle of White.[5] In the evening as we were near the coast of Devonshire there were a great many fishing boats near us so we called out for fish. Three or four let down their boats and brought us what they had. They had not got many. The sea was too rough during night, but the mess I am in — (there are nine of us, it is the largest mess on the ship) — we got two shillings worth. They sold them cheap, so we made a good tea.

On Friday and Saturday, 22nd and 23rd, the sea was very rough. We often sighted land and came very near the same places that we had been at before.

On Sunday 24th. Morning very fine and a few very large Porpoises, or sea swine, came jumping around the ship. There was service on board this morning in the saloon, and in the evening down the main hatch where the married and single women are. As there is no minister on board, the service is conducted in the morning by the Captain, and in the evening by any one who as a like to speak.

Monday and Tuesday and Wednesday it was very rough and just tossed us about the channel. We got a little on, and sighted Portland Point, Start Point, and Lizard Head. There are a great many ships knocking about the channel and cannot get out. We sighted one that was laying beside us in dock which was to sail a week after us.

On Thursday 28th we had a fair wind and sighted Wolf Rock, but in the night it came very rough, and on Friday we were driven back to Lizard Head Light-House. You may think what a disappointment it was to all, when everyone was sick and tired of been tossed about in the channel, and so near of being out of it.

---

[5] I.e., the Isle of Wight

Saturday 30th. The sea very rough but got on a little in our favour. There as always been singing and playing on instruments in the evenings when it as been favourable, but to-night there is an entertainment or concert in the main hatch. (I may just say that the Main hatch is were the Married & single women are. It is the middle of the ship. The forehatch is were the single men are, and the After Hatch were the second class is, and the first class is in the Saloon underneath the Poop.)

A bill was wrote out with the programe on and stuck up in the fore part of the day. The proceedings were gone through just the same as at home.

Sunday 31st. Very calm but wind in favour and all better of sickness. There is service as usual in the saloon presided over by the Captain, but in the evening if the weather be fine it is held on deck, if not in the Main Hatch. Any one can give an address as there is no minister.

On Monday Sept. 1st the wind in our favour and we got out of the channel, about one hundred and fifty miles. Scores of Porpoises came about the ship but not so large as the first lot. The Passengers started to wash their clothes. We can wash when we like on deck but we have to get water best way we can, for it is not nice washing in salt water. All sorts of games were carried on as the sailors had nothing to do for the first time since we started and all was going well.

In the Evening we sighted a Man-of-War ship belonging to England. She had the white ensign at the peak and also signal flags flying below representing the letters G.G.V.J. Upon reference to the Code signal book they knew her to be the Tenedos, twelve Guns, screw steamer.[6] Captain Phillips of our ship at once ordered our official V.P.J.K. to be hoisted in return, by which those on board the Man-of-War would not only know that their own signal had been understood, but at the same time be able to read our name. The Tenedos then asked where from, and with marvellous

---

[6]H.M.S. *Tenedos* was an *Eclipse*-class wooden screw corvette, launched in 1870. She carried three masts, ship-rigged, and was fitted with a ram bow. She seems to have led a peaceful life, and was sold in 1887.

rapidity our answer was run up, London twenty days out. She next enquired where bound, too which we replied Canterbury,[7] and immediately after the Captain signalled, Please report us all well. The Tenedos promised to do so and wished us a pleasant voyage. We thanked and saluted her, by dipping our ensign three times. The distance at which we passed was about four or five miles. Our ship would be no dought reported at Plymouth or some of the channel Ports next day. It was interesting to many of us who had for the first time the opportunity of witnessing a conversation carried on at sea by two ships miles apart by means of a series of flag signals.

Tuesday 2nd. Wind in favour and the weather very fine. The sailors month was up to-day, and the dead horse was made. It was made of straw and bags. It was about the size of a Donkey but very like a goat, only it had a long tail. It was taken to the middle of the ship and put up for sale, [for] which they collected about fifteen shillings. One of the sailors was dressed like an old man with a long white coat and a long beard, made of towed rope. Then the rope was put through a pulley on the end [of the] lower yard on the main mast, and tied to the man and horse as he was on its back. They were then drawn over the side of the ship and swung about for awhile. The rider then loosed the horse from under him and it fell into the sea. He was then lowered down, and then all sorts of amusements was carried on untill very late.

Wednesday 3rd. The wind in our favour. They started to take the observations and to mark them down on a board so that everyone might see the longitude and latitude, and know how many miles we had gone. To-days was Latitude 44°−30′. Longitude 12°−42′. Miles 158.

Thursday. Weather very fine. We are some where on the coast of Portugal, in Lat. 42°−37′. Long. 14°−10′. Distance 133 miles.

Friday 5th. Very fine and going well. The distance was not put up to-day, but every day it was put up I took it down on a paper by itself. So I will not put it in the book as it takes up so much room, only occasionally to let you know (if you look at

---

[7]Canterbury is the district including Lyttelton, New Zealand.

The front page of the *Euterpe*'s Agreement and Account of Crew for the voyage of 1879. This document was the crew's employment contract. Two of the notes read "No spirits allowed" and "The ship shall be considered fully manned with Thirty hands all told."

the map of the World) whereabouts we are at. And the number of miles when I reckon'd them up they are only about fourteen thousand miles.

In the evening the second concert was held. It was in two parts. It commenced at six Oclock, and finished at nine-forty. There were lots of songs but tune had left a good many of the singers.

On the 23rd of August the Engineer had his forefinger taken off with the Condensing Engine.[8] It as been stopped since, untill to-day when one of the passengers took the job.

Saturday 6th. Wind in favour.

Sunday. Very calm. Service as usual. Some of the passengers were fishing. Their was one caught about six pounds weight.

Monday 8th. Very calm. There as often been disturbance about our treatment of provisions for we only got a part of them given to us, for the Coffee, Peas, Rice, Oat Meal, and salt Meat are given to the Cooks. (There are two Cooks.) So to-day when we went to the Galley for our meat there was not one ounce for each. So all went and stormed the Galley, and searched everything but the Cooks said it was all they got from the Mate, and we could not find any more. So we went to the Captain and let him see, so we arranged to see everything weighed out to us.

We have to make our own bread or any thing else we want and take them to the Cooks Galley to Cook them, so they have certain days for every thing. On Sundays and Wednesdays they boil Duffs, and we get Salt Meat one day for dinner and Salt Pork the other, but not on Duff days, and preserved potatoes evey other day. It is not often we can eat the Meat as it stinks so, we just throw it over in the sea and we get Coffee every morning and Burgoo or Poridge one morning and boiled Rice the other, and Peas soup every other dinner time.

Tuesday 9th. We sighted Madeira, and came very close to it. It is very hilly and rises from the sea very like Skiddaw. They have arranged to publish a paper on board Called the Euterpe Times, once a week, to come out on Saturdays. It will only be a

---

[8] I.e., the ship's fresh-water condenser, thought to have been located in her hold abaft the mainmast.

manuscript one wrote for each Cabin.

Wednesday. Very fine. In the evening service was held, and to be held every Wednesday evening.

Thursday 11th. We arranged to hold a Bible Class, On Sundays afternoons in one of the Boats. In the Evening a lad about twelve Years, named Taylor, fell of the forecastle and dislocated his elbow.

Friday 12th. Weather very fine. A notice was put up in the morning that there would be a foot race, at five thirty P.M. between an old man about fifty, and a young Irishman. They had to run five times around the deck. The Old man stripped off and did it in one minute and forty-eight seconds. When the Irishman appeared he was very amusing. Some one had lent him a pair of tight-skins and a black belt. He did it in one minute and twenty-six seconds, so two got him on their shoulders and carried him around the deck.

And then a walking match had to come off between the sailors and passengers. So a Young man in the single cabin walked first. It is about one hundred and fifty yards and they had to walk twenty times around. He did it in eight minutes & thirty-eight seconds. Then a sailor tried but gave in the sixth time around. He was three minutes. So then the entertainment commenced which passed off very lively. They are held on deck when fine.

Saturday 13th. A little breeze. The paper came out to-day, and very interesting it is. We generally go by the number of our bunk instead of the name. I am No. 5, in No. 1 mess. There was a Song in the papers about a young man from London, a mess mate, he is No. 3. It is as follows —

> There is a lively sort of chap,
> Whose down our forward hatch;
> I guess for sea antipathy,
> On board he has no match.
>
> For him a Sea life has no charm,
> He'd sooner be on land;
> He cried to be on shore once more,
> A five pound note I'll stand.

And to our Captain he repaired,
But he replied with reason;
That to desert our noble ship,
Would be the foulest treason.

So No. 3 while here you be,
I'd prove myself a man;
And if of sea life you'r afraid,
Why buy a Dolby Can.

While we were in [the] channel a good many was frightened. After the narrow escape with the Hurunui there was one night it was very rough, and the sailors were calling aloud and an Old Man named Duff thought we were comming in collision and he run up on deck naked and shouted, and a good many followed in their shirts. This sort of thing was done a few times untill every one got tired of it. One chap used to put his Dolby Can on every time, and some times he would have lost the cork and others it would be full of water. So he goes by the name of Dolby.

Three of the Pigs died, and two were dressed for the first class passengers.[9]

Sunday 14th. Very fine service was held on the Poop at 10.30 A.M. Bible class at 2.30 P.M. Service on main deck at six Oclock P.M.

Had an increase. Mrs. Fairhurst gave birth of a Daughter at 11.15 P.M., just as we entered the Tropics. She is in the third cabin.

Monday, 15th. A very large fish came alongside of the ship for a while, it measured about 35 ft. in length. It was said to be a Grampus; it was very like a whale. There were a few flying fish yesterday, the first we saw, but there has been hundreds to-day. They are very small, the largest about [the] size of a small herring. Their wings are very large to the size of the body. They could not fly far, for as soon as their wings got dry they fell. Sometimes they would fall on the ship's deck, and they could not fly off again.

Tuesday, 16th. A sale took place at 3 P.M., Mr. Middleton acting as auctioneer. The articles were of a miscellaneous character,

---

[9]As on earlier voyages, pigs were kept in a pen atop the main hatch.

consisting of Potted Meats, Salmon, Lobsters, Sardins, preserved
Milk, Tobacco, Candles, Dishes, Tins, Wollen and Linnen Jackets,
Hats and Caps, Cheese, Lemons, Sugar, and Leather Laces. The
bidders were very keen especially for Milk and potted Fish. They
went for four times their value. Clothes go very cheap and those
that wants money to drink will sell a good suit for a few shillings
and drink is very dear on board. Some sell their bread and we
can get sixpence for a bit about [the] size of our hand.[10] [sic]

In the evening the Childrens' singing contest came off. After
each Girl and Boy had sung two pieces the prize was awarded
to John Austin. Mr. Duff gave the prize and on ascending the
platform, said, "Ladies and Gentlemen, this boat was made by
a gentleman on board the Euterpe whose name is Mr. Wagstaff.
It is a complete model and the name of it is Nonsuch, bound for
New Zealand." He then handed it to the Boy.

Wednesday, 17th. A very large bird named an Albatross came
alongside of the ship. Also a shark came across the fore end twise.

Thursday and Friday very fine.

Saturday, 20th. Very wet. This is the first wet day we have had
since we left the Channel.

There are two pieces of Poetry in the paper this week. One
is about the little chap that used to put his Dolby Can on every
time he thought there was danger.

> There was a Jolly Grocer,
> The smallest man of three,
> Who went to sea against the wind
> On Board the Euterpe.
>
> But still that Jolly Grocer,
> Of Sea life has no fear,
> For in his bunk confidingly,
> A Dolby he keeps near.

---

[10]Lister refers to the English coinage of his time, in which 12 pence equalled
one shilling, and 20 shillings equalled one pound.

A south by west the Gallent ship,
With well-filled sails kept beating,
T'was hid from sight between the waves,
That waved a fearful greeting. (Hurunui)

But sullen sky and roaring wave,
The Grocer can't alarm,
For ever since he's been to sea,
He's trusted in his charm.

Sunday. Wet. Service as usual.

Monday. Wet. Vessel in sight. The Captain said he thought it was homeward bound so nearly all the passengers had got letters wrote before they saw She was going out.

In the evening sighted another vessel; when we got near, her flags were showing the letters H.G.J.K. She was a Swedish Barque. Foreign Ships don't give their names. She signalled for Greenwich time. She was bound for the Cape, sixty-five days out.

Tuesday 23rd. Morning wet, cleared in the evening. A few ships in sight. A very large Whale came near the Ship for a while and hundreds of Porpoises following it, and turning summersets out of [the] water. [sic] We could see the Whale for miles off, making water spurt up in the air.

Wednesday 24th. Spoke to a Swedish ship, showing letters H.K.Y.G.

Thursday 25th. Spoke to an Italian ship showing letters N.B.M.K., from Cardiff with coals for Buenosayres,[11] forty-eight days out.

Friday 26th. Spoke to an English schooner named Mary Bowen, from Swansea to Cape Town, forty-two days out, letters R.K.H.

Saturday 27th. Wind against us and has been for a few days. There is a piece of Poetry in the papers about the Ship Euterpe. It is as follows:

---

[11] I.e., Buenos Aires

The English schooner *Mary Bowen,* spoken by the *Euterpe,* probably was similar in appearance to this schooner, the *Dispatch* of Garmouth. Contemporary English schooners normally had square topsails, as in *Dispatch,* while American schooners were more likely to carry a full fore-and-aft rig, and perhaps dispense with the fore topmast as well.

The voyage of the Euterpe

A Ship set sail from London Town,
Set sail for a distant land;
Her name was the Euterpe;
Cap't Phillips did her command.

On a Friday night did she set sail
Full glorious shone the stars
And loudly sang and strongly pulled
Her crew of jolly tars.

She anchored off the Gravesend pier
Before she sped her way
And what did happen to her there
Was the Doctor's fault they say.

The Doctor was a jolly man
And well did love good cheer
Perhaps he did not like the sea
I vow he liked good beer.

Oh had that Medicine man been there,
And lingered not o'er wine,
They'd have gone before a glorious breeze
And long since crossed the line.

Eight Bells had struck aboard that Ship
The sound Scarce died away
When the Talford struck her on the stern[12]
And let in light of day.

Oh panic was then rife on deck
And folks rushed to and fro
And Oaths and Prayers & Dolby Cans
Were strangly mixed with woe.

Then back again to London town
Back into dock she went
Before she went again to sea
Full ten long days were spent.

But now they've a med of a different sort
No word I'll say against him
He never goes to roost at night,
Untill he's dowsed each glim.

Though now she's nearly out to sea
The breezes are contrary;
The only merit they possess,
Is that of being airy.

Oh why can't ships let her alone,
And try at least to clear her;
Now *Hurunui,* sure You know,
You should not go so near her.

---

[12]This contradicts Lister's earlier statement that the *Talford* struck the *Euterpe* in the latter's starboard bow.

They beat about for sixteen days,
Of reaching they'd enough,
They reached and tacked before they got,
Past Biscay wild and rough.

But now she's well upon her way
The wind is in her favour
And in a Year or so perhaps
At her journeys end You'll find her.

Moral

The moral of this story is
On friday don't set sail.
Well anyhow then if You do,
Be sure You do not fail.

[No entry was made for Sunday, September 28th.]
Monday 29th. Wind against us.
Tuesday 30th. Wind in favour. We expect to cross the line at midnight. About nine Oclock Old Neptune shouted from under the Bowsprit. (It was one of the passengers who acted Neptune. He was dressed with an old coat and long wiskers made of towed flax.) A good number of the passengers went on the forecastle to see him, and some of the sailors and passengers had the boats full of water, unknown to most of the passengers, and when Neptune had spoken awhile from below the bowsprit, he called for water and those in the boats throw water on the passengers that was hearing Neptune speak. Then they started on all parts of the ship to throw water on all that was on deck and none escaped not even the Captain, only the women that was below escaped. A few in the single mens cabin that was frightened turned into bed to get clear, but about twelve Oclock they pulled them out of bed and took them on deck and gave them a good weting. Only three on board got the customary shave, with tar and slush and scraped with a piece of hoop iron.

Wednesday 1st of Oct. Sports were held to commemorate the crossing of the line. The sailors got holiday for the afternoon. First on the program was a race over the main royal yard. The

110

This is the oldest photograph available of the poop deck and skylight of the *Euterpe*. It is believed that it was taken shortly after 1900, just a few years after she ceased carrying emigrants.

winners were A. Kasson and Purcell who ran a dead heat, time 1 m. 44 sec. Next came the tug of war between ten sailors and ten passengers. The passengers won two out of three times. Third, Foot race, five times around the deck. Fourth, three-legged race. Fifth, was hand over hand, up a tight rope. Sixth, Sack race. Seventh, Carrying buckets full of water on their heads. Eighth, Boys race. Ninth, foot race, boys and Girls. Tenth, last race.

Thursday, 2nd. Raffle of a watch. The sailors were forbidden to take any part in shaving the passengers while crossing the line. But their was one lathered with Treacle and Tar and shaved with a piece of iron, to-night, because he said he would fell the first one who touched him.

Friday, 3rd. Another watch was raffled.

Saturday, 4th. Good breeze. We have been going well since the day before we crossed the line.

Sunday, 5th. Service on the Poop. Sighted an American barque. Signalled to her but they only answered by hoisting her colours.

Monday, 6th. Sighted at 11.45 A.M. a British barque showing letters T.K.B.G. from Rio-de-Janeira, homeward bound. Asked her to report us all well. At 6.30 P.M. spoke to the Coowapie of South Shields, homeward bound.

[No entry was made for Tuesday, October 7th]

Wednesday, 8th. Wether very fine and going well. They took our boxes out of the hold, for the second time since we left London. While they were taken them out, a fight commenced between one of the sailors, and the third Mate. (The sailors and mates are a mixed lot of all nations.) The sailor refused to work after, and he was put in irons.

Thursday, 9th. A Sale took place like the other ones. Sighted an American barque. She signalled for our Longitude which we gave her. In the evening there was a raffle for a revolver.

Friday, 10th. Childrens sports that were posponed on account of darkness on the day of the Euterpe sports, came off to-day, which caused great exitement. The last was a singing contest of Girls and boys, won by W. Taylor. After came off the fifth Concert.

(We crossed the Line in Longitude 24° 38'. The Latitude runs down untill we get to the line, and then it runs up again.)

Saturday, 11th. Very calm. We expected to be out of the Tropics in a day or two, but this has stoped us. In the evening there was a ball on the main deck. Just as it was getting dark two whales were seen going past the ship.

Sunday, 12th. This has been the most memorable day for exitement since we left the docks. The sea was like a great table-land. We could scarcely tell the slight motion, and the water was so clear that we could see a great way down, some said a quarter of a mile. The sun rose beautiful. (It rises and sets very different in the Tropics than it does on land. It has beautiful colours.)

And soon after we could see a whale about half a Mile off. It came up to the ship a few ft. off and blew up twice against the ship and raised its head and back out of water and then made off. He could easily have been harpooned. A little after, two of the apprentices started to bath, but were stoped. After dinner a fine shark came gently swimming around the ship accompanied by his pilots. These latter were from two to eighteen inches long and coloured very like the Mackeral. Some went right before his nose to steer him, and other small fish by thousands followed behind. Several baits were let down to entice the shark to take [a] bite, but he was rather shy for some time. And he kept going around the vessel three or four times within a few ft. so that all could see him. A harpoon was thrown at him, but without effect. He next caught at a bait hung from one of the poop boats, but also inefectual. He took biscuits that was thrown out to him.

At a quarter to five he took hold of one of the baits that was hung from the bowsprit. Some were giving orders what to do to get him up, when another shark caught hold of another bait and both were now fast to the lines and on the point of being hauled up on deck, when all at once, the lines broke and both sharks got away. At the same time another shark was seen comming towards us, but took his departure. After a while he came up. And after tea stronger lines and hooks were got and it was not long before he took hold. They pulled him a little out of water and put a noose around his tail and hauled him on deck, where they cut his tail and fins off and took his inside out. There was such a crush on to see that they threw him over board. He was about six ft., six inches long. There was the sucker fish stuck fast on his back untill he was on deck. They then took it off and kept it alive, for some days.

In the afternoon there were lots of large porpoises and flocks of very large birds floating on the water. There were also a good many Albatrosses. These are the largest sea Birds. The sun set most splendid.

Monday, 13th. We had a little breeze.

Tuesday, 14th. A good wind. We got out of the Tropics at night. The Captain says he never knew so coole weather going through the Tropics.

Wednesday, 15th. Very fine. Saw a Dolphin fish. A line was just down and he took hold and was pulled out of water, but got away again. It seemed to be about nine pounds weight, it was the nicest colour of any I have seen. The rest of the week passed over very calm.

[No entries were made for Thursday, October 16th, through Saturday, October 18th.]

Sunday, 19th. At 8.45 A.M. sighted a British Ship in Lat. 29° 20′ South, Long. 26° 7′ West. Named Baron Blantyre of Greenock, 1623 tons, commanded by Captain Wilson, bound from Cardiff to Calcutta with cargo of coals, 44 days out. It came in sight in the morning, on the same tack as we, caught up to us at 11 Oclock and in the evening left us out of sight.

Monday & Tuesday & Wednesday [20th-22nd]. Very calm, scarcely moveing. In the night of the last named day, the top Gallant Yard broke from its fastings [sic] and came down with a run on the upper top sail. It was made partly fast and in the morning was lowered down (that is, on Thursday morning). And one of the spare spars was commenced with to make a new one.

Also an Albatross was caught with bait and line. It measured from tip to tip across the wings, ten ft. Its plumage was a beautiful white colour with slight tints of Primrose, its body about the size of a Swan.

[No entry was made for Thursday, October 23rd.]

Friday, 24th. A strong breeze with rain. In the evening came a gale, all sails were taken in, but the sea run mountains high, and the ship rolling heavily so that the main yards were dipping in the waves. In the night it was awful; we could not get a wink of sleep. Boxes, Tins & Boots were rolling about. Some messes lost all their week's stores. The hatches were closed, but the water came through fast, so we were in a nice mess. No one could stand without haveing hold of something. We scarce could go on deck, for the sea was comming over like mountains and we often got wet through.

Saturday morning as soon as it was daylight we got up to look after our things. Some were looking for their boxes, others for their Tins. I found one of my cogs [at] the other end of the cabin, and I think if I had had boots I should have lost them, for I was the only one that wore clogs on the ship. Some of us went up on deck to wash as usual, but while we were washing she rolled down on one side and we all went rolling about the deck. Their are no exceptions between passengers and sailors for falling. One woman was carried near the length of the ship with a wave, and another named Mrs. Owen fell and broke her leg in the cabin, comming out of her bunk.[13]

Sunday, 26th. No wind, but a great swell. The ship rolling heaveily, could not have service.

Monday, 27th. We are now halfway on our Journey in Lat. 38° 50′ and Long. 12° 11′. Distance to-day, 202 miles. To look back it seems a long time, it being eleven weeks since we started the last time, and we have been liveing near thirteen weeks on board Ship. Yet the time has gone over so very quick it looks to be very short. We cannot expect anything but a long passage for it takes a gale to drive her along, and then they are obliged to take in sail or they are carried away, or the ropes broken.

There has been a few Cape Pigeons caught. They are a nice bird with spotted wings and not quite so large as a Duck. There has also been a few Molly-Hawks caught. There is scarcely any difference between them and the Albatross, but a little smaller.

Tuesday, 28th. Going well. Some of the Passengers are helping to get the Yard made. A Patagonia Hen (or Stink pot) was caught, measuring six feet across the wings. They are a dark brown bird and about the size of a Turkey.

[No entry was made for Wednesday, October 29th.]

Thursday & Friday [30th and 31st]. Going well. A Cape pigeon caught itself by getting its wings entangled in a line.

Saturday & Sunday, Nov. 1st and 2nd. Very calm in the morn-

---

[13]We shall encounter the ill-starred Mrs. Owen and her brood again towards the end of this chapter.

ing. Service held in the saloon. In the evening [service] was held in the main hatch.

Monday, 3rd. Several Molly-Hawks caught. Also Mutton Birds, they are about [the] size of a duck, a grey-colour; also some Whale Birds, they are about the same size.

Tuesday, 4th. We passed the Longitude of the Cape of Good-Hope. In the afternoon, several Shoals of Grampuses, and the largest whale we have seen, came very near.

[No entries were made for Wednesday and Thursday, the 5th and 6th of November.]

Friday, 7th. A few birds were caught and amongst them was a dark grey Albatross, and a Patagonian Hen.

Saturday, 8th. Going well.

Sunday, 9th. I supose it will be Martinmas Sunday. Yet it is never mentioned on board.

Monday, Tuesday & Wednesday [10th-12th]. Going well. Caught several Molly Hawks.

One of the second class passengers stole some fresh potatoes, and the one that was least expected, for sometimes he conducted the meetings on the Sunday evenings. And as the Editor of the paper is in the second class, they will not put anything [negative] in the paper that happens in the Saloon, or second class. So some of the single men in the forard hatch-way started an illustrated paper and they had his portrait drawn and had him in four acts. First act was getting the potatoes out of a case and taking them in a pie to the Galley. Second part was the Cook holding the drag fork up and asking him where he got them, and he offering the Cook 2s. 6d. The Third was the Trial, and Jury sitting. Fourth he was giving out a hymn on the Sunday night he got the spuds. They were posted up on deck every day, and they caused much amusment.

Thursday, 13th. The sea began to be rough, squals coming rapid, took all sail in.

Friday, 14th. Squals continued and by the afternoon the sea had got very high. About four Oclock the jib sail was carried away. They were going to repair it, when the third mate struck one of the English sailors and a fight took place, and the mate got his face cut severely and both eyes swelled up so that he had to grope his way to his berth.

The sailors had scarcely got to work with the jib, when a sea came over and carried away part of the bulwarks, and top of the main Hatch, and sky lights where the Married people are, and their Cabin was filled two feet deep with water so their boxes were floating about.[14] Their hatch was soon covered over with canvass. And then they had to cut the [partition] into the single men's compartment, to let them get out, and the passengers turned too to take water out with buckets which was soon done. The second cabin also got their share with water. So the forard Hatch was the only place that escaped. The Doctors stores were all spoiled. The Married and Single women has to come out of their cabin by the young men's cabin.

Saturday, 15th. Some of the passengers were engaged to repair the hatch.

Sunday, 16th. They got a doorway put up, but only a temporary one, to last the voyage, so they only can get up by it when it is calm. Service morning and evening as usual.

Monday, 17th. A shoal of Porpoises came about the ship.

Tuesday & Wednesday [18th-19th]. Nothing particular.

Thursday, 20th. In the evening about six Oclock, two Whales came along side and passed us, rising at intervals out of the water. They seemed to be about 40 ft. long.

Friday, 21st. Several Molly Hawks and a very large Albatross were caught.

Saturday, 22nd. In the Evening a concert was held in the main hatch.

Sunday, 23rd. Service as usual.

[No entries were made for Monday, November 24th, through Thursday, the 27th.]

---

[14]As mentioned elsewhere, the married people and single women of steerage were quartered in the 'tween decks amidships; the single men on that deck forward; and Second Class on the deck aft. Temporary partitions divided the three groups.

Friday, 28th. Nothing particular this week. Sighted a Vessel but a long way off, and a few birds caught.

In the evening a concert was held in the Main Hatch, the largest that has been. You will think that the time passes away dull on board ship, but it is not on board the Euterpe, for at nights there are Concertinas, Tin Plates, Bone Natters, Fiddles, & Fifes. And since the Top of the Hatch and Sky lights were carried away the sky light reflectors were made into Tambourines.[15] So there are playing, singing and druming going on untill about twelve Oclock. I am sure if we were on land they would think we were all heathens. For Number one and two Messes have formed a band. They named it the Tin Plate band.

Here's a piece of Poetry in the papers about it.[16]

The Tin Plate Band

At night soft strains of music,
Was sommus with their tones; [sic]
Tones distilled and sweetly called,
From Tin plates & Pork Bones.

The music swells it rolls it peals,
The harmony is grand:
From platters & preserved meat Tins:
Used by the Tin Plate band.

There's dancing singing to the tune
It has a skilled conductor
Who's famous chief of the tin plate band
Its founder and conductor.

---

[15]The skylight referred to was not the one on the poop deck, but apparently had been erected over the main hatch. Like the partitions, this was probably a temporary structure for the emigrants.

[16]The ship's newspaper was probably written by hand and posted on a bulkhead. Lister calls it a "manuscript" on September 9th.

Unlike a petted child of art
With nobles for protectors
[He] has made himself the tin plate chief
By playing tin reflectors.

Saturday, 29th. They have taken the Mizen and fore royal Yards off, also the Mizen cross sheet. The weather is a good deal warmer, for we have been in cold weather since we left the Tropics. It is very cold comming past the Cape of Good Hope & it is very cold opposite the Cape Horn, which is the most southern point of America. We saw a few Ice-bergs floating past. For out here further we go south, colder it is, & further North warmer.

[No entry was made for Sunday, November 30th.]

Monday, December 1st. Going well.

Tuesday, 2nd. In the evening a disturbance took place and carried on nearly all night so we got no sleep.

[No entry was made for Wednesday, December 3rd.]

Thursday, 4th. A deputation consisting of two men from each Cabin waited upon Cap't. Phillips, for the purpose of presenting him with an engrossed Testemonial expressing the thanks of the passengers towards him during the voyage from London to New Zealand. The address which is in German Text [Gothic script?] is as follows:

To Captain Phillips

We passengers of the Euterpe wish to testify to the kind and considerate manner in which you have discharged your duties and the readiness you have displayed to make our Voyage to New Zealand as pleasant as possible. Now that we are close to port we beg to tender you our hearty thanks for your kind and obliging conduct, and our good wishes for you and yours in the future.

Captain Phillips in reply to the deputation said, "It is very gratifying indeed to me to receive the testimonial at the end of a somewhat long voyage; though with God's help a few days should now bring us to land. It would add one more to the many

This view looking up and aft from the saloon reveals a painting of the muse Euterpe on the after end of the skylight. Facing it from the forward end of the skylight was a rendering of the coat of arms of Liverpool, *Euterpe's* first home port.

SAN DIEGO MARITIME MUSEUM FILE PHOTO

simular Testimonials which I have received since the year 1864, as since then I have taken near upon 2000 passengers to New Zealand. Many who have gone out there to settle permanently make it their business to come down to port when they know I have arrived. I hope you will all succeed in whatever you undertake and will never regret, for I do not think any one will have cause to regret if he is only willing to work and be able to do so.

"I appreciate this expression of your gratitude very much and am only sorry I was not on deck to receive it. If I had known I should not [have] been in the deshabille in which you now see me. I hope you will express my thanks to all your fellow passengers and [say] that I appreciate this address very much, and that none of you will have cause to regret this long journey. Sea life at the best is very different to shore life. We have been favoured with fine weather in this part of the world, for it is not always that we have such a run of fine weather and such good winds as we have been favoured with lately."[17]

A Pig was killed for the passengers to have a treat of fresh Pork.

[No entry was made for Friday, December 5th.]

Saturday, 6th. Very calm. The paper came out as usual.

Life on the Ocean Waves

But enough of the grub & let me recount
How Mary Ann's absence we had to surmount
We have pots to wash up & Puddings to make
Knives & Forks to keep clean & damper to bake
The floor of the Cabin to scrape & keep clean
It's this recreation that's made me so lean.

Those Plum Duffs that we've made, by jove they
    are fine
A sweet reminescence whenever I dine
We made them with biscuits crushed up into crumbs
We made them with Treacle,[18] we made them
    with Plums
We made them with Sugar, raw candy & Hard
A spoonful of limejuice, a little chopped lard.

With some fat of the Pork cut up very small
With a handful of flour I think that was all
Except some potatoes to make it boil light
Yet land lubbers think they know how to cook
Just waite for a nautical Cookery Book.

---

[17]Captain Thomas E. Phillips had first sailed in the *Euterpe* on December 23rd, 1871, on a voyage from London to Melbourne. His last voyage of 10 in the ship left London for Wellington on October 9th, 1882, and returned to Liverpool on March 1st, 1884.

[18]"Treacle" was a common British term for molasses.

Sunday, 7th. Very calm, scarcely moveing. And Albatroses and Molly Hawks were very nice swimming around the ship. At dinner time we got fresh pork roasted and fresh spudds which went very high for a change. In the afternoon several shoals of Porpoises came near the ship's bows. One shoal was the nicest we have seen. Their heads and about a foot on their tails was white and the other part red. They were piebalds. There were several harpooned but they got away; their flesh was too soft. The first one that was struck at, the harpoon pulled its inside out, it made a stream of blood, and the others followed it. It very soon turned on its back and died. The others soon eat it up.

In the evening a nice breeze sprung up. We are about 100 miles from the Snares and near 500 from Port Lyttelton.

Monday, 8th. A head wind.

Tuesday, 9th. In the morning a fine species of Seal came around the ship several times, and crossed under the bowspritt. It often raised its head and neck out of water. And when the Maltese sailors *wistled* it would stop and look around and come near the ship. It had a long neck and head much like a Greyhound, and a brown colour. Some of the sailors tried to harpoon it but failed.

The water is of a different colour here, much like what it is near land. The last Sheep was killed in the afternoon.

Wednesday & Thursday [10th and 11th]. Head wind continues, and we are only tacking to get by the Snares. We are all well accustomed to putting the ship about and pulling the sails up, for we have had quite plenty of practice.[19]

Our provisions are rather scarce now, and they only give us a day's rations out at a time. So some of the passengers are at work making snares to catch rats. There are thousands of rats and a few of the passengers makes Rat Pies. They skin them and then puts the shoulders and legs into a dish and puts a piece of paste on it for a Pie.

---

[19]This interesting entry implies that the passengers assisted the crew in tacking ship and taking in sail. Such may well have been the case, as *Euterpe's* logs list but 15 seamen for one voyage.

Friday, 12th. Sighted the Snares when all were well pleased to see land again, for the first time since we left the English Channel.[20] The Snares are high rocks in two seperate lots. One lot is near 500 ft. high, and the other 200 ft. Both together is about 5 miles in length, they are not very broad. Nothing grows on them but sea weed. It is a fine place for birds to build. It is breeding time now with them and there are thousands flying about. There is no one to disturb them. They are very easily caught from the ship with a hook and bait. Sometimes the passengers caught as many as thirty Albatroses and Molly Hawks in a day. They kept the skins and cured them to make muffs with.

In the evening a Concert was held in the main Hatch so I will give the programme.

Mr. Attreed in the chair
Opening, "Auld Lang Syne" by the Company
Song, "Pour Out the Rhine Wine" — Mr. Hartley
    "   "The Young Recruit" — Miss Attreed
    "   "Won't You Buy My Pretty Flowers" —
        Mr. H. Middleton
    "   "The Land is Now In Sight" — Mr. Bell
    "   "If We Only Had the Holding of the
        Reins" — Mr. Nance
    "   "Early in the Morning" — Mr. Attreed
Solo (Violin) — Mr. Chapman
Song, "Royals Three" — Mr. W. Middleton
    "   "Tom Brown" (assisted by the Tin Plate
        Band) — Mr. Beecroft
    "   "When We Were Boys Together" —
        Mr. Rayson
Duet, "Twine the Lily with the Rose" —
        Mrs. Fairhurst & Miss Hawthorne
Song, "Scots Wha, Hae" — Mr. Millan
Recitation, "The Maniac" — Mr. Skinner

---

[20]Lister omits the sighting of Madeira on September 9th.

Song, "Katey's Letter" — Mrs. Ellis
  "   "When I Took My Nance to Church" —
          Mr. Mayfield
Solo — Mr. Chapman
Song, "In This Wide World of Sorrow" —
          Mrs. Fairhurst
  "   "The Little Church Around the Corner" —
          Mr. Chapman
  "   "The Misses Took a Sly Glance at Me" —
          Mr. Foat
Recitation, "The Sexton" — Mr. Skinner
Song — Master Taylor
  "   "The Daide of Loch Lomond" —
          Miss Hawthorne
Reading, "Vat You Please" — Mr. Thompson
Song — Mrs. Attreed
Closed with "God Save the Queen"[21]

Saturday, Sunday, Monday and Tuesday [13th-16th]. [We have] only been tacking against a head wind but passed the Snares, and sighted Stewards Island,[22] but had to tack again to get around the Traps. These are three rocks about two feet out of water, with breakers going over them.

Wednesday & Thursday [17th and 18th]. Doing very little. The Birds have nearly all left us. The Mother Carey's Chickens have followed us all the way from Madeira. They fly like a Swallow, but they are a little larger. There was only one Albatross following to-day and they shot it with a revolver.

Friday, 19th. Sighted the Main Land, *Otago*, got a nice breeze but a thunder storm came ahead, so we had to put about ship.

Saturday, 20th. A nice wind, we keep very near the coast. Saw Port Chalmers and Dunedin.

---

[21] The titles clearly show the influence of the English music hall. Awash in sentimentality, with occasional comic relief, such entertainments leavened the rigors of many an emigrant voyage.

[22] I.e., Stewart Island

Sunday, 21st. A gale came on but wind in favour. The Cap't. durst not let it go for fear of the bowsprit giving way, so we had to hove too. There were many birds about to-day and a few were caught. They are [a] darker colour to any we have seen. We sighted two vessels. One had her Mizzen mast carried away, but they were both leaving us.

Monday, 22nd. A good wind, only 80 miles to go. They have brought the Tow ropes up.

Tuesday, 23rd. A nice wind. [We] went very close to the Banks Peninsula. We could see a few fires burning, clearing scrub. We expected to get in but [were] disapointed; our old luck, a head wind.

Wednesday, 24th. A head wind, but only about 15 miles off. Signalled to two coasting steamers but [they] did not answer us. We saw a good many different sort of birds.

We got up very close to the opening in the afternoon and a steam tug and a Pilot came and took us in. We anchored about four Oclock. The land seemed very pleasant, and it was very warm. It is the warmest *Xtmas* Eve I ever felt, for it is [the] middle of summer. The Harbour is a fine inlet, but I had to ask where Port Lyttelton was, for we only could see a few houses, and they looked very pretty on [the] side of a hill and plenty of trees around them. There was a little steam tug came and brought letters, and a Doctor & Inspector, but as we had no illness on board, our names were just called over, and anyone who wanted to go ashore could go. A great many went but I stayed untill next day which was *Xtmas* day.

Thursday, 25th. And a few more [passengers] and I went ashore in the morning before breakfast, by a little steam Tug.

Lyttelton is a pretty little place, [and] stands on the side of the hills. And nearly all are wooden houses built a little distance apart, and not built close together like they are at home, but nearly every house stands on a quarter or half acre section, with the exceptions of the Towns where the shops are. They are built rather closer.

I took the train to Christchurch. The Carriages are very different to what they are at home for there are no doors at the sides.

We get in at the end and there are seats on both sides so we can walk right through the train & step from one carriage to another, and there are only second and first class carriages, and it is two pence a mile. And the trains go very slow.

Leaving Lyttelton we go through a Tunnel about two miles long and then it opens out into a nice level country. It looks very nice as everything is in full bloom.

In Christchurch everything seemed to be very quiet as it is a Holiday untill after New Year. It seems rather queer to have Xtmas in [the] middle of summer when fruit is ripe.

Christchurch stands on a square and the streets run parallel one with another, and the four streets which are outside of the town and enclose it in, are called the Belts East, West, North, & South. They are double the width of the others; they are two chains wide, and [each] has a row of trees growing in the middle.

There are no names on the streets and no guide posts so places are bad to find out. The houses are nearly all wooden houses one story high. And most of them looks very pretty all painted, and trees and flowers growing in front of them. There are only a few that are built of stone such as the Post office, and Custom house and Museum, and Bank of New Zealand, and Cathedral. They are fine places. There is only one statue. There are a few fountains, for there is plenty of water. It runs up the artisian pipes about three feet out of the ground.

There is also a nice clear-water river [that] runs through the town, named Avon. It is about twelve or fourteen yards wide and runs very smooth. So Boats go on it nicely. The Town is all level and the land about it is swampy.

So here ends my journey to the other side of the world.

The End.

To John Bragg Lister
Little Broughton
Carlisle, Cumberland
England

I know there will be plenty of mistakes but whoever sees them
will likely know how to correct them. G.J.L.

When you and Father have read it, Please send it to Bros. at
Flimby, and then you can let whoever you like see it. G.J.L.

A POSTSCRIPT TO THE LISTER DIARY

In 1978, Irene Cressey Lister, the wife of George James Lister's
grandson, published a short article in the *New Zealand
Genealogist*. The article concerned her research into George James
Lister's life and his voyage in *Euterpe*.

Mrs. Lister recounts that George was born in Great Broughton,
Cumberland, the son of John Lister and Sarah Bragg Lister. His
date of birth is not given, but it would seem to have been in the
1850s or early 1860s. From the conclusion of the diary, we know
that he had at least one brother, John Bragg Lister, who was living in England in 1879, and he may have had two or more other
brothers, judging by his last postscript. His father was still living
at the time of his voyage, although no mention is made of his
mother. Interestingly enough, his diary was sent to his brother
John, suggesting that his relationship with this brother was closer
than with other family members.

Before he left Cumberland, George Lister was betrothed to
Elizabeth Ann Leece of Whitehaven. She soon followed him out
to New Zealand, perhaps in the following year, and they were married at Dunedin in 1881. In 1882 they settled at Clive on Hawke
Bay, North Island. The marriage resulted in 10 children, and a
large clan of Listers eventually prospered in New Zealand.

In May 1978, a great-grandson of George Lister's visited San
Diego. He walked the decks of the old ship his forebear knew
so well, and presented her current owners with a copy of the diary.

"Lyttelton Harbour—Schooner running for the Tide, 1878" by J. Gibb.
COURTESY OF AVON FINE PRINTS LTD., CHRISTCHURCH, N.Z.

LETTER OF ALEXANDER M. OWEN

Christchurch, New Zealand
29th December, 1932

Mrs. Belle J. Benchley, Executive Secretary
The Zoological Society of San Diego[23]
San Diego, California

Dear Madam:

I was very pleased to learn about the old "Euterpe," now the "Star of India". . . .

Now my task is difficult, to remember details. The sailing date I cannot recall, but the day was Friday. We left East India Dock, mother and we four boys (my father was in N.Z.), on Friday and hadn't got far up the Thames when the steamer "Telford" ran into us and made a nasty hole just above the water line. Two tugs came alongside and towed us back to the docks, where we arrived on Sunday. I remember the excitement of getting off the ship and taking the train to Clapham, where the grandparents lived and what a fright we gave them, as they had heard no news of the collision.

I think it took a week to get mended and, after many more "Goodbyes" we started again and got to the English Channel. (We were nearly three weeks battered about with head winds in the Channel.) Also the ship "Ben Venue"[24] passed us so closely in a fog that she carried away our stay lines. I remember the sailors letting them loose so the mast would not be strained. I well remember also the sudden backing of the sails and the shuddering and thud of the ship. This cracked part of our bowsprit. (By the way, the "Ben Venue" was wrecked — went ashore at Timara afterwards.)

---

[23] The owners of the ship at that time

[24] Owen differs from his brother Ernest (in the following letter) and George Lister in his name for this ship, both of the latter naming her the *Hurunui*. His mention of *Euterpe*'s cracked bowsprit, however, jibes with a reference by Lister on December 21st.

The next trouble was with adverse trade winds, which drove us close to the coast of South America and we could not get away. Had a narrow escape once when we were all sent below and battened down.

My mother, about this time, had the misfortune to break her leg one particularly rough day when she was thrown down. She had a terrible time.

We fellows were packed tight, six in a cabin; had to do our own cooking; very little flour and much hard dog biscuit [sic], grated into the flour and a few raisins, made a fair pudding. The salt junk, we couldn't eat. I remember one of our chaps going about with a horrible lump of fat pork hanging to his watch chain. But in spite of the rough living, we were all healthy and had plenty to do. Two of the six took it in turns to be cooks and others to do the cleaning of the cabin. I was very proud of making a cap out of canvas with a peak to it. It lasted the voyage and that was about five months.

I cannot remember the number of days, but I think it was 120 or 122.[25] We got quite expert helping the sailors. It all helped to pass the time away. By the way, as we were running short of provisions, some of the fellows actually made a rat pie. I wouldn't go near it. Fortunately, we had a fair supply of tinned stuff with us.

At last, on the 24th of December, 1879, I think it was a Wednesday, we crawled into Port Lyttelton. They had given us up. I shall never forget the first sight of the little wooden houses on the hills. We had not seen wooden houses before. What a strange, empty place it looked to us Londoners, used to rows and rows of ugly brick houses. Lyttelton at last.

The health officer passed us. My father met us, much relieved to know we had arrived. Then the journey through the Lyttelton tunnel to Christchurch. Arriving at Christchurch station, we were rather taken back to learn that we must avoid certain streets as the Orangemen and the Hibernians were rioting.[26] I don't know

---

[25]Shaw Savill records show the voyage took 125 days, land to land.

[26]This refers to Protestant Irish and Catholic Irish settlers, respectively.

what about. We were taken to a friend's house and, after tea, the friend had to leave us as he was on special constable duty. To make up, on Christmas morning, a warm summer day was a novel experience.

I have written to my brother Llewellyn, who reminds me of the "Rat Pie." It may be of interest to know that he wrote his first waltz and called it the "Euterpe Waltz." By book post, I send you a copy. He has composed other waltzes, but the first — the "Euterpe" — was the most popular.

Alexander M. Owen

A bemused Llewellyn Owen surrounded by the ladies of his "Estudiantina" band. Owen became a well-known musician, composer and instructor in New Zealand, but he never forgot his boyhood days in the *Euterpe*.

PHOTO COURTESY OF GWYNETH OWEN

LETTER OF ERNEST F. OWEN

March 28, 1948

100 Dean St.
St. Albans
Christchurch
New Zealand

[To American historian Harold Huycke]
Dear Sir:

In our local paper, "The Star-Sun," I read an article requesting any news or information about the sailing ship, the "Euterpe." My mother and her four sons, Alexander Milsted, age 16 years; Sidney Charles, age 15; Ernest Frederick, age 11; & Llewellyn, age 9, left the East India docks, London, in the ship "Euterpe," Captain Phillips. I am the third son & am writing from memory of some incidents on that voyage.

We left the docks August 1st, 1879. Arriving at Greenwich[27] we were all awakened one night when another ship collided with ours, smashing the bows of the "Euterpe" almost to the water line. It was necessary for us to be towed back to the docks to be repaired. This work took some weeks until we finally set sail for New Zealand. Owing to contrary winds it took us three weeks to clear the Channel.

Early in the voyage my mother suffered a severe accident.[28] During a severe rolling of the ship my mother was accidentally knocked down by a fellow lady passenger, & broke her leg. This necessitated her being laid up for the entire voyage.

---

[27]According to Lister, the collision took place at Gravesend. This correlates with government records for the period. Greenwich is actually *up* the river from East India Dock, whereas Gravesend is down river and the normal moorage for emigrant ships.

[28]Lister refers to this on October 25th. However, the accident may have occurred earlier in the voyage, as Ernest Owen states. Interestingly enough, Lister, Alexander Owen, and Ernest Owen each give a different account of how the accident happened.

132

The voyage was very slow owing to some defect, so we were told, of one of the masts. Food became very short & all who might remember those early days will recall its lack of variety. As a boy I can well remember the excitement among the passengers when a rat pie was brought from the galley & the crowd of passengers who followed it from the cook house to the fore part of the ship where the single men bunked.[29]

We had a weekly newspaper which my eldest brother, Alexander, laboriously wrote out. He had always been a beautiful writer even to the time of his passing at nearly 80 years of age.

Captain Phillips was much respected by all & he & the crew did all they could to help & entertain the passengers, of whom, if my memory serves me correctly, there were about 300.

It was a very tedious voyage & took just on 5 months before we reached Lyttelton Harbour, New Zealand.

One or two things stand out in one's memory after such a long voyage. I was very proud of a yacht made for me by one of the crew, Bob Bessington. We were about 3 weeks around the "Needles" before we finished our voyage on December 24, 1879.

My father, Alexander Owen, who had come to New Zealand a year before us in "The City of Perth" sailing ship, & who with many others began to think our ship had been lost, came out to meet us & a very happy reunion it was.

In the English channel we nearly had another collision with the sailing ship—I think it was another Shaw Savill boat— "Harunui."[30] During a dense fog she suddenly appeared right in front of us. By clever seamanship she just managed to scrape by, while we could have almost shaken hands with her passengers who with us were, I am sure, expecting a disaster.

My eldest brother, Alexander Milsted, passed on when within a month of 80 years of age. He was for many years secretary for the M.E.D., the Municipal Electrical Department of this city. My

---

[29]I.e., to the 'tween decks below the fore hatch.

[30]The *Hurunui* at that time belonged to the New Zealand Shipping Company, as stated in that company's history and by Lister.

second brother, Sidney Charles, who passed earlier, was a school inspector of the Education Board here. My younger brother resides in Dunedin & is a retired school master & was a well-known musical instructor. All three of my brothers were organists, the eldest Alexander sometimes relieving Mr. Bradshaw at the Christchurch Cathedral.

I cannot recall anything further at present. I am nearly 80 & one's memory is often not quite as keen as in former years. Hoping these items may be of use to you,

I am Sir,
Yrs. respectfully,
E.F. Owen

Waltz

for the
PIANOFORTE
by

LLEWELLYN OWEN.

Composer of
The Royal Cambrian Barn Dance. ETC.

PUBLISHED BY
LLEWELLYN OWEN.
SCHOOL ROAD,
WEST EYRETON,
CANTERBURY
NEW ZEALAND.

Part Two:

THE SAILORS

Euterpe is fast to the Shaw Savill & Albion Company wharf at Port Chalmers, New Zealand. This was a favorite spot for photographs of the company's ships. After Shaw Savill's merger with the Albion line in 1882, their sailing ships were painted in this "gunport" style. The upper strakes of the hull were black, the "gunports" black on a white band, and the lower strakes were French gray. The boot top underneath was red. This was a popular style for deepwater merchantmen from the Blackwall frigates of the 1830s to the early 1900s. The date of the photo is unknown, except that it was taken between 1884 and 1898.

SOURCE: ALEXANDER TURNBULL LIBRARY, WELLINGTON, NEW ZEALAND

VII.

THE SAILOR'S LOT

The second part of this book concerns itself with the working life of *Euterpe's* sailors. As the 1870s waned into the 1880s, the emigrant tide to New Zealand and Australia waned also. The New Zealand government put the brake on its earlier policy of assisted immigration, due to pressures generated by an overrapid expansion of the colony's economy. Meanwhile, Shaw Savill, feeling the pinch of competition, amalgamated with its long-time rival, Paddy Henderson's Albion Line of Glasgow. This produced the Shaw Savill & Albion Co. in 1882. Their main remaining rival was the New Zealand Shipping Co., formed in 1873.

All this led to increased emphasis on cargo to and from New Zealand. Typical cargo outward bound might consist of pig iron and consignments of manufactured goods; the usual cargo homeward bound to England was wool.

Crews had to be leaner, more efficient. The twilight of working sail was fast approaching, as more and more steamships chuffed out on the sea, their coal smoke staining the skies a greasy black.

Sail could still be profitable on the longer cargo routes, and this was not to change for some time. Also, despite the better working conditions in steam vessels, many sailors considered them beneath contempt. "He's left the sea and gone into steam" was a comment applied to an ex-shipmate who'd seen the future's light in the blaze of fireboxes.

Square-rig crews were a mixture from all nations and the *Euterpe's* were no exception. These men are on board the British ship *Scottish Admiral* at San Francisco in 1892. Besides the "Limeys," there are present a Russian Finn, a Norwegian, a Frenchman, a German, a Canadian and an American. The two in the middle of the front row are apprentices. In the second row, the carpenter sits with his trusty mallet. The three men wearing caps in the third row are, left to right, the sailmaker, mate, and second mate. The man on the far right of the third row is said to be the "doctor." The rest are A.B.'s and O.S.'s.

SOURCE: THE ROBERT WEINSTEIN COLLECTION,
NATIONAL MARITIME MUSEUM, SAN FRANCISCO

There was not yet any shortage of able-bodied seamen. And where there was, masters did not hesitate to connive with crimps to dump any sort of human flotsam on board. San Francisco was notorious for this business, although other ports — Liverpool and Hamburg among them — were not far behind. Every major port in the world had its sailortown or red-light district where such scourings might be found. In London it was Limehouse and Whitechapel; in Hamburg, the St. Pauli district; and in San Francisco, the hell-roaring Barbary Coast. Thus by hook or by crook a crew was cobbled together.

What manner of men were these? Many were highly skilled seamen, the like of which will never be seen again. Others had never been aboard ship; they rolled into port, as the saying had it, with straw stuffed in one ear and hay in the other. In age they ranged from their teens to old age. (It was not unknown for a hungry man past his prime to dye his hair with shoe-black, so that a mate might think him years younger.)

* * * * * *

"A.B." and "O.S." — these acronyms separate the sailor of experience from him with little or none. The A.B. was the Able-Bodied Seaman. As the lore put it, he was required to "hand, reef and steer." And he had to do a great deal more. He had to be ready to risk life and limb at a moment's notice; to tumble out of a bunk and go aloft off Cape Horn — where ice took the skin off a man's hands as he climbed the shrouds. He had to be able to move swiftly to a line on deck or aloft in a sheeting hell of water and wind. He had to know exactly what to do with that line, when — and if — he got to it.

There is an unfortunate modern tendency to romanticize this man. Actually, from the photographs that have come down to us, he was a rather runty individual — ill-nourished and looking it. He was tough as a line of rawhide, however. He could take a beating again and again. "Drowned a hundred times; back for more."

140

The common A.B. of the Victorian era had no formal education. Like the scrap-cat found among alleys, he was simply lucky to stay alive to his majority. Many a sailor of the time we discuss could not read and write. He sometimes sought out a better-educated man to write any news he had to send home — if there was any "home." The average sailor, it must be said, lived for little more than the next carousing spree in the next port. Money meant nothing to him; if he had it, he spent it till it was gone.

The labor of the sailor was endless. If work aloft did not occupy him, holystoning the deck might do. If a long and arduous passage had been concluded, more brutal work awaited him in unloading cargo. Always he was at the mercy of the mates and bo's'n, whose active eyes quickly spotted the idle hand and relaxed posture, and set about turning these items to the ship's benefit.

An exceptional A.B. might be named Boatswain. The bo's'n was the leading petty officer of the deck, and was often seen in charge of groups overhauling rigging, painting ship, caulking

The fo'c'sle of the *Star of India* as it appears today. When the ship was the *Euterpe,* its appearance was much the same. This was the habitation of 15 to 25 sailors for months at a stretch — their "home away from home" at sea and in port.

PHOTO COURTESY OF ROBERT SHARP

seams, repairing tackle, and any other work that needed to be done on deck. He had his own space, the bo's'n's locker, located in the very bows of the ship at the 'tween decks level, where his gear was stowed. Typically he was a rugged individual, and as vital to the ship as the carpenter.

The O.S. — "Ordinary Seaman" — was like as not a vagrant drafted aboard at the last minute. Basil Lubbock, an A.B. in a four-masted barque in 1899, on a voyage around the Horn, spoke bitterly of an O.S. named Higgins, that he was an old man unfit for service, that he tumbled into the scuppers at the first sign of a swell, that he was useless aloft. Such was the lot of the O.S. — a man or boy who had a lot to learn in a harsh environment.

Above these common seamen existed the "idlers" — those who were mature enough (or cagey enough) to find a softer billet. Idlers did not work watch-on-watch at sea; not for them, the misery of four hours' sleep, four hours' labor, four hours' sleep, repeated endlessly. For they had acquired some skill which set them apart. The idlers in *Euterpe* included the carpenter — an indispensable man who had many tasks in the daytime, but who slept (mostly) undisturbed at night. A carpenter in a square-rigger had to be a man of vast skill and aptitude; he was constantly worried over and set-to by the mate; he was oiling, carving, shaving, shaping, honing, filing, planing, and bending the ship back into shape. The ocean battered her; the carpenter set her right.

Along with the carpenter in skill came the sailmaker. If a ship was lucky enough to carry one, the sailmaker sat out on a hatch-cover in the sunshine and bent to his work. His needle and palm were never idle; his patches parted the sky in zig-zag rows on the royals; his handiwork might save a ship.

After the carpenter and sailmaker came lesser lights. Among these were the cooks. The cooks were often roundly hated. They were commonly older or disabled men who worked in the deck-house galley, laboring over an iron range in all weathers. The emigrants cobbled together messes which took their rations to the galley. There fights sometimes erupted, as the Lister diary makes clear. Few sailors or emigrants were ever really satisfied with what they got from the cooks; complaints about food and the way it was prepared probably outnumbered all other complaints *en masse*.

It should be said in the cooks' defense that the rations they had to work with were not of their own choosing; furthermore, they were certainly conscious of the fresh-water limits. *Euterpe's* condenser sometimes broke down, and even when working correctly, it was not a Niagara. All hands were allotted three quarts a day—which seems adequate.

Along with the cooks came the stewards. The steward at sea was akin to the butler or footman on land; he waited at his betters' table, poured his betters' wine—and when his betters were seasick, he tidied up after them. A steward saw much and kept all within his own counsel. He took care of Cabin Class ladies and gentlemen, waited upon their creature comforts, picked up after them, made things spotless before them. He eased their lives, in short. That was his job.

The life of a steward could be hazardous. If he had to slog through a torrent on deck from galley to saloon, that was also part of his job. (A good steward could keep a silver tray balanced while grappling his way along a lifeline in freezing water up to his chin.) After negotiating green-water decks, the steward had to spit the fish out of his mouth and serve his betters as if all were at the best dining room in London. That was part and parcel of his job.

Euterpe carried three stewards on the voyage of 1884. The pecking order was "Steward," "Second," and "Passenger." Between them they attended to first and second class, and served the master and first mate. (Steerage fended for itself.) The pantry off the saloon was the head steward's little domain, where he might be found polishing the Cabin Class silver. His underlings, meanwhile, would be set to cleaning cabins and a multitude of other tasks.

Above the "idlers" came the officers. On their skill and knowledge depended the lives of hundreds of human beings. The average officer in *Euterpe* seems to have been a good one. Captain Thomas Phillips was especially admired among the emigrants—but others were also respected.

There is no modern equivalent to command under sail. This sort of leadership called for split-second decisions combined with the accumulated wisdom of centuries. It was a lonely job — far more lonely than the modern skipper's. Frequently a captain "made an isolation of himself" for months at a stretch. In a crisis, everything would depend on his judgment and nerve.

Masters were not made out of molds. For the merchant service, there was no university to manufacture them. Most commonly, they made themselves.

The average officer had signed an indenture as a lad, gone to sea as an apprentice (15 was a common age), learned his business from the scuppers up, and by sheer tenacity succeeded to command. The minimum period of apprenticeship before sitting for a mate's certificate seems to have been three years. The "school" was rigorous: climbing aloft under a withering blast of ice-sleet off Cape Horn could concentrate the mind wonderfully on the task at hand.

By degrees a man worked his way up to his Certificate of Competency as Master. The next step after apprentice was normally second mate. (Some ships carried third mates — including the *Euterpe* in the 1870s. In the 1880s, due probably to a more stringent economy on the part of her owners, she did not always carry thirds.)

After passing an examination made up by the Board of Trade, the new officer with his "ticket" tried to find a berth. If times were good, that wasn't much of a problem; if times were hard, the officer might take a berth lower than he was qualified for — or even ship out as an A.B.

The second mate occupied a rather peculiar position. Although he wore the blue uniform coat and visored cap of an officer in the British Merchant Service, socially he was regarded as neither fish nor fowl. He normally did not bunk in the saloon cabins like the master and first mate, but was quartered elsewhere. In his work he possessed not the lordly authority of the mate, much less the god-like status of the captain. Unlike the mate, he was expected to doff his coat and work alongside the crew if necessary. The more assertive men in the crew regarded him as a virtual equal—yet he was not one of them, either. He had to make the best of his lot and hope that he could succeed to a "first ticket" before long.

Here at last we come to the nail, the peg that held it all together. Despite his relatively high status, no one in the ship worked harder than a good first mate. In the logs that follow, the reader will see this borne out again and again. The first mate was the captain's strong right arm and the most visible officer to the crew. Among his multitude of tasks, he was responsible for seeing that the ship was sailed according to the master's orders. If the master was not on deck, the first officer—or simply "mate"—might decide on sail to be set or taken in, maneuvers such as tacking or wearing around the wind, and all aspects of sailing the ship. In effect, he was the captain when the captain was not present.

It normally fell to the mate to enforce discipline in the crew and, if necessary, among the passengers. If a crime such as theft was committed, he carried out searches for stolen goods and hauled suspects before the master for questioning. He was in charge of rations for the emigrants, and had to be vigilant about these and the fresh-water supply. He supervised the crew directly in their work, paying particular attention to the carpenter, whose work was often vital to the ship's endurance.

Every day at sea, he "shot the sun" with his sextant (as did the master) and wrote up the log at noon for the preceding 24 hours. (In port he wrote up the log in the evening of each day.) The ship's log was a important legal document which had to be kept accurately. Owners, magistrates, the Board of Trade and insurers such as Lloyd's of London all might want to examine it after a voyage. There was a certain prescribed form for keeping a log; a mate was expected not to litter it with too many personal observations. On the other hand, it had to be detailed enough to present a full picture of the ship's operation.

It sometimes happened that the master would keep his own log. But the log kept by the mate was the "official" one; the master read each entry and signed it daily.

When at last all perils of the sea had been surmounted and

the ship came into port, the hardest work of all began. This was the unloading of all cargo, the loading of new cargo, and readying the ship for sea again. Unloading cargo was rugged physical labor for all hands, and again the mate was in charge. Commonly in the colonies, *Euterpe* had to anchor out in a bay or harbor, there being no wharves or piers to accommodate her.

Using her "cockbilled" yards as cargo booms, the crew put in long days of grueling work to get all her cargo over the side and into lighters. The work went on six days a week, with (if the mate was decent) Sundays off for rest. The men began work early in the morning and often went on for hours after dark. They worked in the rain and sleet as well as the hot sunshine. (Some lightermen in New Zealand would stop work at the first sign of rain. The mate of *Euterpe* would then make acid comment in the log and drive his own men all the harder.)

Not surprisingly, the highest number of injuries among the crew occurred while off-loading. Hands were smashed, limbs mangled, eyes torn. Also not surprisingly, the men began to desert — one, two, or three at a time, they slipped away. The mate was usually not terribly concerned. There were always hungry men on the beach who longed to see England again — or merely to eat again. If all else failed, one simply sent to a local crimp and told him how many bodies were needed. Granted, this material might include derelicts, cripples, swagmen and various bits of gaol-bait — but then what choice might a hard-pressed mate have?

After off-loading cargo, it was a point of honor with the mate to get the ship cleaned up as soon as possible. Actually, this process began before the ship reached port. No matter what kind of battering she had been through, officers ordered sailors to spruce up her topsides and paint the sides of her hull — if weather permitted — prior to sailing in. Not all ships were this strict, but the *Euterpe* under Captain George E. Hoyle was.

After the clean-up, of course, there was a new port to shift round to and a new cargo to load. Getting the stuff into the hold doesn't seem to have been quite as arduous as getting it out, but it was difficult enough. *Euterpe's* normal homeward cargoes from

New Zealand were wool and tallow. The former came in bales and the latter in casks. These were not unduly hard to handle, compared to the "pigs" of iron and odd-shaped manufactures she had hauled out.

Thus, the life of the mate. In reality he was a master-in-training. Someday when he made command, all his hard-won experience would come in handy.

In the following pages, you will meet a most extraordinary man — "William Paterson Mate" (as he signed the log). In his own words, he will tell you of the daily life of a working mate in sail. A fine, hard-driving officer if ever there was one, Paterson may stand as a model for the best in all of *Euterpe*'s afterguards.

We also present excerpts from the personal log of Captain George E. Hoyle. Hoyle was new to the *Euterpe*, but he seems to have known his business thoroughly. (Walter Savill, sitting in his cavernous office at 34 Leadenhall Street, London, would have made sure of that.)

As for *Euterpe* herself, the falling-off of the emigrant trade by the mid-1880s made her less of a passenger vessel and more of a working cargo ship. Passing her 21st year, she found herself forced to compete with newer ships and the rise of steam. She was an aging iron lady, now. Only her sailors' sweat and blood made her turn a black dollar.

"REGULATIONS FOR MAINTAINING DISCIPLINE"

These were promulgated by the Board of Trade for the Merchant Service and posted on board all British merchant ships. This particular copy was posted on board *Euterpe* on April 21st, 1872. The following is the list of offenses and punishments:

		Amount of Fine
No.	OFFENCE	or Punishment
1	Not being on board at the time fixed by the agreement	Two Days' Pay

| 2 | Not returning on board at the expiration of leave | One Day's Pay |

| 3 | Insolence or contemptuous language or behaviour towards the Master or any Mate | One Day's Pay |

| 4 | Striking or assaulting any person on board or belonging to the Ship | Two Days' Pay |

| 5 | Quarrelling or provoking to quarrel | One Day's Pay |

| 6 | Swearing or using improper language | One Day's Pay |

| 7 | Bringing or having on board spirituous liquors | Three Days' Pay |

| 8 | Carrying a sheath-knife | One Day's Pay |

| 9 | Drunkenness. First Offence | Two Days' half allowance of provisions |

| | Ditto. Second Offence | Two Days' Pay |

| 10 | Neglect on the part of the Officer in charge of the watch to place the look-out properly | Two Days' Pay |

| 11 | Sleeping or gross negligence while on the look-out | Two Days' Pay |

| 12 | Not extinguishing lights at the times ordered | One Day's Pay |

| 13 | Smoking below | One Day's Pay |

| 14 | Neglecting to bring up, open out, and air bedding, when ordered | Half a Day's Pay |

| 15 | (For the Cook)—Not having any meal of the Crew ready at the appointed time | One Day's Pay |

16	Not attending Divine Service on Sunday, unless prevented by sickness or duty of the Ship	One Day's Pay

16   Not attending Divine Service on
Sunday, unless prevented by
sickness or duty of the Ship .... One Day's Pay

17   Interrupting Divine Service by
indecorous conduct .... One Day's Pay

18   Not being cleaned, shaved, and
washed on Sundays .... One Day's Pay

19   Washing clothes on Sunday .... One Day's Pay

20   Secreting contraband goods on
board with intent to smuggle .... One Month's Pay

21   Destroying or defacing the copy of
the agreement which is made
accessible to the Crew.............. One Day's Pay

22   If any Officer is guilty of any act or default which is made
subject to a Fine, he shall be liable to a Fine of twice the
number of Days' Pay which would be exacted for a like
act or default from a Seaman, and such Fine shall be paid
and applied in the same manner as other Fines.

A NOTE ON PAY

As to pay in the *Euterpe*, Ordinary Seamen started at about
£2, 10s per month in this period. The A.B. got only a few shillings
more — perhaps £2, 15s. An average wage for a cook was £4 per
month, while the sailmaker got £5. The carpenter actually made
more than the second mate — £5, 10s vs. £5, 5s. The first mate
might command £8 per month. Far above them all ranked the
master, who usually negotiated his pay with the ship's owners.
A master worth his salt might collect £20 a month or more. It
was scarcely a fortune, but if he saved it carefully, he might have
enough to live on in his old age. That was more than most sailors
could manage — so they kept going back to sea until they died
in harness. (Source: *Sail to New Zealand* by David Savill,
London, 1986.)

VIII.

THE VOYAGE OF 1884-85: GEORGE E. HOYLE, MASTER, AND WILLIAM PATERSON, MATE

1884-85: A MOMENT IN TIME

The world continued to change—too fast for some; not fast enough for others.

Transportation was steadily becoming more mechanical; these were the last years in which sailing ships would outnumber steam vessels in the British Merchant Service. Coaling stations spread around the world, and steamers were slowly gaining in endurance and range. They now dominated the trade to India, via Suez. Reliable transatlantic passenger service was coming into its own, with liners like Cunard's *Oceanic* and the crack new *Servia*.

Even the Royal Navy—grizzled bastion of arch-conservatism—began to part with its beloved sails. The two most recently built iron battleships—*Neptune* and *Inflexible*—had been rigged as a barque and a brig, respectively. But the sails were almost useless.

They could not move the armored hulls through the sea unassisted, and were damaged by smoke and cinders from the ships' stacks (not to mention the increased risk of fire in the rig). These years saw the sails on both ships removed, to be replaced with "military masts" and fighting tops. The next pair of battleships—the *Agamemnon* class—never carried sails at all. A turning point—and a break forever with the ships of Drake, Rodney and Nelson—had been reached.

There were other reverberations in naval circles during these years. The torpedo boat was the latest rage, complete with self-propelled torpedo. At the same time, there was a harking back to one of the earliest naval weapons—the ram. Ram bows would be designed for warships until well into the early 1900s—despite little evidence of their utility.

As steam was crowding out sail on the seas, other forms of mechanical power were advancing on land. In Germany, a man named Daimler devised a strange contraption—a carriage that ran without a horse. Powered by a tiny gasoline engine, his buggy could reach the mind-boggling downhill speed of 20 miles per hour!

In America, the first telephone poles were going up. Boxy, wooden-cased "'phones" began to sprout on the walls of homes and offices. In the summer of 1884, much was made in the U.S. press over the fact that Maggie Blaine, daughter of Republican presidential candidate James G. Blaine, received the news of her father's nomination via the new marvel.

Despite the cascade of technology (a word, by the way, not yet coined), life went on as usual for most people. The United States was in the grip of the most feverish presidential contest yet seen—the "Dirtiest Election" between Republican Blaine and Democrat Grover Cleveland. The mud-slinging on both sides probably attained an all-time low, with Blaine accused of stock frauds and Cleveland forced to acknowledge fathering an illegitimate child. Blaine tried to link the Democrats closely with the Roman Catholic Church, but this strategy backfired and cost him the election. Cleveland took the oath of office on March 4th, 1885, to begin a four-year term marked by many reforms.

On July 28th, 1885, another American leader would pass on: Ulysses S. Grant. Despite the scandals surrounding his presidency, Grant became a popular figure in his final years. He wrote his famed *Memoirs*—still one of the best autobiographies ever penned—and the pallbearers at his funeral included former Confederate general Joseph E. Johnston and Union general William T. Sherman. The deep and bitter scars of the Civil War were at last beginning to heal.

As the Republicans yielded power to the Democrats in America, so did the Tories to the Liberals in England. William Gladstone replaced Disraeli as Prime Minister in 1880, holding the post until 1885. It was the "Grand Old Man's" second of four stays at 10 Downing Street. Gladstone differed from Disraeli in not wishing to extend the British Empire further than was necessary. He was loath to sink large sums of money in imperial schemes, and even more loath to send British troops into foreign misadventures.

Just such a misadventure occurred in 1884-85. A vast revolt flamed up in the Sudan (or, as they spelt it then, the Soudan). The Sudan was corruptly ruled by Egypt, which—for reasons involving the Suez Canal—was closely watched over by the British.

The leader of the rebellious desert tribes called himself the Mahdi, "The Expected One," a prophet destined to deliver all Islam from the grip of unbelievers. The Mahdi drove the Egyptian garrisons back to Khartoum, where their resistance stiffened with the arrival of General Charles Gordon—soldier-of-fortune, religious mystic, and idol of the British public.

Gordon quickly scrapped his instructions from Gladstone to evacuate the Sudan, and did his utmost to defend Khartoum. This put Mr. Gladstone squarely upon some very painful horns: he was furious at Gordon for not obeying his orders—yet he could hardly leave the popular general to his fate.

A British army went to Egypt, thence to advance at a crawling pace up the Nile to Khartoum. The rescue expedition was, alas, 48 hours too late: on January 26th, 1885, 60,000 of the Mahdi's shrieking dervishes breached the walls of Khartoum and began to massacre its 8,000 defenders and 35,000 inhabitants.

Gordon died on the steps of the palace, reported by an eyewitness as turning his back on his assailants with contempt.

And back in Britain, Gladstone's political career was — for the time being — as dead as the headless corpse of Gordon.

Europe remained at peace, but tensions continued to build. Italy had joined Germany and Austria-Hungary in the Triple Alliance of 1882. This was regarded as another master stroke by German Chancellor von Bismarck. The always-vigorous German people were rapidly building the most advanced industrial state in Europe. Germany began to compete with Britain and France for colonies in Africa and elsewhere. The German merchant marine — hitherto noted only for its smallness — began to grow at an astonishing rate. The old Kaiser, Wilhelm I, was fading away; but in the wings stood his grandson, soon to become the second emperor of that name.

France was also flexing her muscles, with French troops moving into Indochina (modern Vietnam, Laos, and Kampuchea). A prolonged struggle ended with the French dominant — and with the native peoples seething for generations at their rule.

The French also sent expeditions across the Sahara to establish control over enormous areas of west and central Africa. Meanwhile, the Germans, Italians, and Belgians were scrambling for their own places in the African sun.

In Russia, Tsar Alexander II had ended his reign in the fiery blast of an anarchist's bomb. He was succeeded by Alexander III, a massive, bearded bear of a man, who if anything bore down harder on his people than the previous ruler had done.

All these things were in the papers and the minds of people in Glasgow during these years. But on the River Clyde below the city, two men had more immediate concerns. They were the master and first officer of a ship named *Euterpe*. In the spring of 1884, they prepared their iron vessel for her next trip around the world.

GEORGE E. HOYLE, WILLIAM PATERSON,
AND THE *EUTERPE*

This voyage was certainly among *Euterpe's* ruggedest. Difficulty and hardship beset her, both in damage sustained to the ship and in deaths and injuries.

It began badly enough. Attempting to leave the Clyde with a largely Scottish crew on April 9th, 1884, she collided with the steamer *Canadian*. After feverish repairs, out she went at last on the 19th. The winds were light and not very helpful until she found the westerlies in the latitude of the Cape of Good Hope. From there on, gale after gale struck and bowled her along. Before reaching New Zealand she would encounter a full-blown hurricane. The good side of this coin was that she made her fastest-ever passage out, 104 days port-to-port.

Death would stalk this passage, too. The first casualty was a stowaway, a Scots lad named John Campbell. Shortly after leaving port, Campbell and two accomplices were rousted out of their hiding place by Mr. Paterson, the mate. The three were set to work with the crew, which numbered but eleven A.B.'s and four O.S.'s. Two months later, Campbell was aloft in the main rigging when he lost his grip and plunged one hundred feet to the deck. Three days later, they buried him.

The following month, barely a week before reaching Port Chalmers, Francis D. Orr, a first-class passenger, died of the dropsy (i.e., edema). He too found a grave in stormy seas.

On August 1st, with an adverse wind plaguing them, they towed into Otago Bay. They had to anchor off the shore and begin the grueling work of off-loading cargo. No labor is more arduous to the sailor.

The ship's master was George Edward Hoyle, born of Wisbeach, new to her this trip. He was 38. Thomas Phillips, her veteran skipper, had transferred to the *Zealandia*, a swift iron clipper specially designed for carrying emigrants.

The *Euterpe's* first officer, William Paterson, was a Scot. He was 30 years old, born of Ayr, a mate in *Edwin Fox* the last time out. We know little about his life except that he was diligent,

Front page of the Agreement and Account of Crew for the *Euterpe*'s voyage of 1884. Some late additions read: "No Cash shall be advanced abroad or liberty granted other than at the pleasure of the Master", "Passengers not to be molested on crossing the line" and "No slops allowed."

meticulous, and an acute observer. One of his primary duties lay in keeping the ship's log. His careful Spencerian script reveals a man of some education — as do his judicious entries. To an unusual degree for a mate, Paterson describes the working life of *Euterpe* in considerable detail. Consciously or unconsciously, he adds small human touches which illuminate the ship's inhabitants.

By contrast, Captain Hoyle hews to a crabbed scrawl in his personal log. He gives us little but latitudes, longitudes, weather and the set of the sails. Still, his brief jottings serve to corroborate those of Mr. Paterson. (All spellings and abbreviations are as in the originals.)

The voyage continued with the ship leaving New Zealand for the return journey to England via Cape Horn. She cleared the colony on December 2nd, sailing finally from Napier, and arrived at East India Dock, London, on April 11th, 1885 — one year plus two days after her first troubled departure from Glasgow.

"LOG OF THE 'EUTERPE' "

"LOG of the 'Euterpe' of Southampton, Tons 1197, Commanded by Geo. E. Hoyle, On a Voyage from Glasgow to Otago [Port Chalmers] N.Z. — thence to Napier, Towards London. Commencing April 9th 1884, Ending Sat. 11th April 1885."

Captain Hoyle's Log
Wednesday: April 9th 1884
Left Queens Dock at 11.45 am in tow of "Flying Hurricane" — Pilot Clelland in charge — when approaching Linthouse saw a steamer aground about 100 yards ahead — our helm was put "hard a port" but ship refused to answer helm and we struck the steamer — the "Canadian" in the stern carrying away our bowsprit — figure head — Knight heads and all head gear more or less damaged — returned to Glasgow for repairs.

Mr. Paterson's Log
Wednesday 9th April 84

At 6 A.M. Started with shore gang & cleared up decks got chain up and ranged 14 fths[1] chain on both sides, Stevedores passing in the Passengers luggage etc. finished at 9.30 A.M.

At 10.30 A.M. cast adrift & proceeded through the Dock in tow of the "Flying Hurricane" ahead & the "Flying Cloud" astern. Pilot Clelland in charge. Cleared the Dock heads at 10.45.

When approaching the Lint House saw a Steamer about 100 yards ahead evidently aground with her bow on the South shore and her stern across the stream. Our helm hard to port the ship started to answer it then stopped (11.10 A.M.) and drove straight into the stern of the Steamer "Canadian" breaking our bowsprit in halves also the martingale & bobstays with all the gear attached broken and damaged. Hausepipes, Figure head, Knightheads, blocks deadeyes sheets and downhauls all damaged by the wreckage, our Hauser being also badly chafed. We at once backed out with the Tug alongside, canted head up stream & returned to Glasgow mooring at Yorkhill Buoys head & stern. Crew clearing up the wreckage, etc.

> Master. Geo. E. Hoyle [signed]
> Mate, William Paterson

Thursday at 12.30 A.M. Hauled alongside the wharf at Yorkhill mooring head up stream, finished up at 2 A.M.

9 A.M. Started and washed decks.

11 A.M. Nilson A.B.[2] Johnsen A.B. Cotter A.B. Ek A.B. Holm A.B. McAulay A.B. cleared ashore without leave. Baird, Hunter, Reid, Kirk, & Oliphant A.B.s [and] Menzies, Mackway, Shaw, Jones, O.S.s[3] remaining to work. Mr. Guthrie's gang sending down stays etc. and unshipped the broken bowsprit. Crew that are working sent to Sailors home to live. Forecastle undergoing repairs.

---

[1] I.e., fathoms. Fourteen fathoms equals 84 feet.

[2] An "A.B." meant an Able-Bodied Seaman, or fully qualified sailor.

[3] An "O.S." was an Ordinary Seaman, partly qualified or unqualified.

Friday 11th

Crew employed cleaning ship Fore & Aft scrubbing paint work etc., shore gang prepareing to receive new stays.

Saturday 12th

All hands that are available cleaning the paintwork and geting every place cleaned up. Carpenters and Iron workers working all night last night.

The house flag chosen by Robert Shaw and Walter Savill in 1858. It can be seen at the main truck of *Euterpe* in two of her earliest photographs. This had been the original national flag of New Zealand, in use from 1834 to 1840. The design was influenced by the Royal Navy's White Ensign, with its red Cross of St. George on a white field. The canton was another red cross on a blue field, with white six-pointed stars. It proved a popular banner and was one of the best-known flags of the British Merchant Navy for over one hundred years.

Sunday 13th

No work doing this day Sunday. Weather very fine and clear throughout. Winds Easterly.

Monday 14th

Carpenters and Ironworkers started at 3 A.M. working hard. Inquiry held at Messrs. P. Henderson's Office before Mr. Gallows.[4] Capn. Brown,[5] Five of crew examined and their deposition taken. Mr. Clelland [and] Mr. Bell pilots also examined.

Tuesday 15th

Crew clearing up main hold. Carpenter toming [? sic] off the cargo in the tween decks. Shore gang setting up the Fore stays. Carpenters labourers riveters & iron workers all at work at the damage, night & day.

Wednesday 16th

Another inquiry held at Messrs. [space left blank; presumably the same location as the first inquiry]. Collins, Boson,[6] Reid A.B., Almon & Chadwick apprentices were this day examined along with pilots Clelland & Bell.

New bowsprit shipped at 4 P.M. Crew overhauling brace blocks halyard blocks etc. etc.

Thursday 17th

Carpenters and repairers all at work night & day until the job gets finished. Mr. Guthrie's shore gang setting up Fore topmast stays etc. Hauled the Ship down the wharf to a berth lower to allow a steamer to get in, to the crane.

Friday 18th

Rigged out the Jiboom and rove all the stays guys & backropes martingale stays and everthing having been renewed. Cleared up decks at 4 P.M. having got every thing in order & ready to make a start.

---

[4] Evidently a local magistrate. (And a very appropriate name, too.)

[5] Apparently the skipper of the *Canadian*

[6] I.e., the boatswain

Friday contued at 4 A.M. [i.e., Saturday morning]

In the morning at 12.10 the carpenters finished up and unrigged their stages, having completed the job to the entire satisfaction of all concerned.

The crew who have been at work all the time are Baird A.B., Reid A.B., Hunter A.B., Kirk A.B., Oliphant A.B., Menzies O.S., Mackway O.S., Shaw O.S., Jones, O.S. Cotter, Nilson, Johnsen A.B.s and Ek A.B. joined yesterday morning, the others not turning up. Capn. Hoyle shipped two more in their places. 2nd Mate, Carpenter, Boson, Cooks & Steward being all at work since we returned.

Saturday

The full list of crew who joined this morning are

Captn G.E. Hoyle	Master
W. Paterson	Mate
M. Wylies	2nd Mate
Collins	Boson
McNichol	Carpenter
J. Douglass	Steward
J. McKinlay	2nd Steward
Ja. Auld	Passenger Steward
Alex. Gavin	Cook
Thos. Whally	Ast. Cook
J. Reid	A.B.
J. Baird	A.B.
G. Hunter	A.B.
J. Kirk	A.B.
M. Cotter	A.B.
D. Oliphant	A.B.
B. Johnsen	A.B. [Norwegian]
W. Ek	A.B. [Swedish]
C. Nilson	A.B. [Swedish]
J. Menzies	O.S.
H. Jones	O.S.
J. Shaw	O.S.
G. Mackway	O.S.

Livingstone   A.B.
Collins   A.B.[7]

Saturday 19th April
Draught of Water 21 ft. 6 in. aft 21.4 Ford.

Started at 4 A.M. and cast adrift the moorings. At 5 A.M. let go and swung ship's head down stream, with the Tug "Flying Owl" ahead and the Tug "Flying Spear" astern. Pilot for River in charge.

At 5.45 passed over the Rock and touched ground very heavy two or three times. Passed Dalmuir lt. house at 6.10 A.M., Bowling at 6.30, Dumbarton Castle at 7.10 A.M., Port Glasgow 7.30 A.M., Princes Pier Greenock at 8 A.M. Came to anchor in Gourock bay at 8.30 with 45 faths. chain at the hause Starboard anchor. Swung ship and adjusted compasses.

At 11 A.M. hove short, at 2 P.M. Hove up and proceeded, Pilot Bell in charge, towed by the "Flying Owl." 3.30 Passed *Cloch* Lt. house. 5.30 Abeam of *Cumbrae.* 8.15 Ailsa Rock abeam. 9.20 Pladda lts. abeam. 2.15 Let go the steam tug. Set all available Sail.

Sunday 20th April
At Midnight loosed all sail and set the three lower topsails, at 2.15 A.M. let go the steamer and made all available sail. Light northerly breeze & fine clear weather. . . .

1.30 P.M. St. Johns lt. house bearing NW dist. about 8 miles. Light airs and calms continue. . . . At 10 P.M. Rockabill Light in range bearing WSW.

Midnight. Light steady breeze from the Eastward, clear wr. Found three lads who had stowed themselves away in the coal hole, their names are Neil Smith, John Campbell, & Hugh Duff.

Monday 21st April
At 3 A.M. Rockabill lt. bearing WNW dist. 7 miles.
At 10 A.M. not being able to weather Codling bank lt. ship,

---

[7]Not the same man as the boatswain

Tacked & Stood off until 11.30, then tacked & stood to the S.W. Wind gradually freeing.

11.45 Codling lt. Ves. abeam. . . .

6.40 Blackwater light ship abeam. Moderate breeze & fine clear weather continues throughout.

Tuesday 22nd April 84

. . . At 2 A.M. Rounded the Combeg light ship and stood in for the Hook, N.W. by after compass. At 5.45 Landed pilot Bell off the Hook in a Waterford cutter. . . .

At 10 A.M. Minehead light House bearding WNW. Wind continues light. . . .

A British pilot cutter. This one is the Falmouth Cutter No. 8, photographed in the late nineteenth century.

This log contains 12 Hours and ends at Noon.[8]

ON THE LOOK-OUT

Menzies	Cotter
Barr[9]	Collins
Kerr[9]	

LANTERN HUNG OUT.

Sunset to Sunrise

Wednesday 23rd April 84[10]

Light to moderate breeze with fine clear Wr. All sail set.

The ketch *H.F. Bolt,* built at Bideford in 1876. After 1870 the ketch became a popular rig for small fishing craft in the waters around the British Isles. It is likely the *Euterpe* saw many of these.

SOURCE: NATIONAL MARITIME MUSEUM, LONDON, U.K.

---

[8]I.e., the entry for April 22nd ends at noon on that day.

[9]Barr and Kerr are not listed on the crew roster of the 19th. It is likely they were passengers assisting the crew, as Lister recorded emigrants doing in 1879. Each lookout watch lasted two hours between 8 P.M. and 6 A.M. Henceforth the names are listed each day.

[10]Henceforward each day's entry ends at noon of the date above that entry, and reports events of the preceding 24 hours. Thus the entry for the 23rd, for example, begins at noon on the 22nd.

8 P.M. Light airs with slight easterly swell. Old Head of Kinsale bearing WNW dist. 15 mil., from which we take our departure.

8 to 10.30 Ship lying becalmed off Kinsale light. Then had a light breeze from the S.E.

Midnight Passed a fleet of fishing boats. Light S.E. breeze & clear Wr.

At 6 A.M. Seven Heads bearing NNW. Brisk & freshening breeze & clear.

Thursday 24th April 84

Begins with a brisk breeze & fine clear Weather. Stowed anchors and cables. . . . Bent the Crossjack, and rove all the royal gear etc. etc. . . .

Friday 25th April 84

PM Begins with light baffling airs and calms. 2 P.M. Squally with rain.

10 P.M. Wore Ship to Sthrd on the starbrd tack, to clear Ship to leeward. Wind veering West rain at times.

AM Heavy rain to 2 A.M. . . .

Carpenter employed at cabin table. Crew overhauling royal halyards, blocks & gear etc.

Dist. per Log, 58 Miles.[11]

Saturday 26th April 84

PM Very light Easterly airs & calms. Sent aloft the main royal yard and set the sail. . . .

AM At 1.30 A.M. a fresh breeze came away from the N.W. in a squall. Set all sail.

Carpenter repairing fore royal yard, oiling etc. Crew clearing fore hold, stowing away ships stores etc. . . .

Dist. per log, 116 Miles.

Sunday 27th April 84

PM Begins with strong breeze and passing squalls accom-

---

[11]I.e., the distance covered from noon, April 24th, to noon, April 25th.

panied with rain. Cleared up decks in the afternoon.

9.30 P.M. Stowed M. royal, & the top gallant Staysails. Heavy squalls with rain at times.

2 A.M. Heavy rain, wind veering to N.W.

3.30 Wind moderating, set all sail. . . .

Noon Fresh & steady breeze from the NW.

Dist. per Log, *219* Miles.

Monday 28th April 84

9 P.M. Heavy squall with rain. Handed main royal and the M. & miz. topgallant Staysails.

AM Brisk & steady breeze & fine clear weather. Vivid flashes of lightning in the Eastward.

Carpenter employed at sundry small jobs. Crew variously employed, set up Fore topgallant & royal stays & backstays, crossed the Fore & Miz. royal yards.

Noon One of the Steerage passengers, Mr. Robert Drysdale, reported having had a pocket book stolen out of a black bag. The pocket book contained a cheque for £30, nine pounds in gold & 2 letters of recommendation.

Tuesday 29th April 84

Commences with a brisk Northerly breeze with fine clear Weather. All drawing sail set.

2 P.M. Searched all the steerage passengers' berths and baggage for the stolen property, but could find no clue to the recovery of the Money. W.P.

8 P.M. Wind gradually decreasing. . . .

Towards 4 A.M. wind veering to the N.W. freshening. All sail set. Weather clear and fine. . . .

Noon. Brisk breeze with fine clear weather.

Dist. per Log, *189* Miles. . . .

Wednesday 30th April 84

P.M. Brisk breeze & fine clear weather. Setting up Guys, etc. Repairing Main topgallant sail. . . .

Midnight. Brisk breeze & very clear weather throughout. . . .

A.M. Crew overhauling blocks & gear, etc. Repairing old mainsail & main topgallant sail, finished both ready to bend.
Noon. Slightly overcast, brisk breeze.
Dist. per Log, *176* Miles.

Captain Hoyle's Log
Thursday, 1st May
Fresh NNE wind and cloudy weather; a barque in company.
Noon: Fresh NNE wind and overcast; shifting sail.
Lat. 31°13′N—Long. 21°54′W.[12]

". . . a barque in company." At the end of the Age of Sail, a barque meant a vessel square-rigged on the fore and main, fore-and-aft rigged on the mizzen. In 1901 the *Euterpe* was reduced to a barque rig by the Alaska Packers.

SOURCE: NATIONAL MARITIME MUSEUM, LONDON, U.K.

---

[12]Unlike Mr. Paterson's log, which ran from noon to noon, Capt. Hoyle's log seems to have been written late each day, to cover that calendar day. *Euterpe's* position on this date put her a little over 200 miles southwest of Madeira.

Mr. Paterson's Log
Thursday 1st May 84

Commences with slight hazy weather and a brisk breeze, gradually clearing. Bent the second mainsail.

8 P.M. Made fast all the Fore & Aft canvas. Wind northerly with slight drizling rain at times. . . .

A.M. Banking up to the NE wind freshening.
Carpenter fitting up oil room in deck house.

Captain Hoyle's Log
Friday, 2nd

A ship & barque in company. . . .
Week's run 1319 miles.

Mr. Paterson's Log
Friday 2nd May 84

Commences with a brisk breeze & very pleasant weather, all the square sail set.

Overhauling a large ship, also a Barque, which are to windward. . . .

Captain Hoyle's Log
Saturday, 3rd

1st flying fish seen.[13]
8 P.M. Light NE wind and fine. Held Concert.

Mr. Paterson's Log
Saturday 3rd May 84

A brisk and steady breeze with all square sails set. Bent the topsails fore & aft & main topgallantsail etc. . . .

Carpenter at oil room. Also cleaning steering gear and oiling yards etc.

Crew overhauling blocks etc. Sent down topsail lifts fore & aft and fitted downhauls.

All appearance of the Trades. Flying fish about.
Dist. per Log, 181 Miles.

---

[13]During the night of May 3/4, the ship crossed the Tropic of Cancer.

Captain Hoyle's Log
Sunday, 4th

Exchanged signals with ship "SAN STEPHANO" of Yarmouth, Nova Scotia, from Cardiff for Rio Janeiro — 11 days out. Also signallised steamer bound North.

Mr. Paterson's Log
Sunday 4th May 84

P.M. Moderate breeze with very fair weather throughout, all sail set. . . .

Spoke the Ship "San Stephano" 11 days out from Cardiff bound to Rio. . . .

Monday 5th May 84

1 P.M. Sigld. A German Steamer which passed two miles to leeward. . .

A.M. Wind continues steady and freshening a little towards 4 A.M. The "San Stephano" still in the same position as she was yesterday, on our lee quarter. . . .

Noon. Brisk and steady breeze. "San Stephano" crawling ahead & to windward.

Monday 5th May Civil date

At 1 P.M. Owing to information received from Mr. Almon 3rd Mate[14] that he had seen one of the Steerage passengers, Frank Ross, trying to put a chisel, or something, back secretly into the carpenter's room, yesterday, Sunday, and it being reported by one of the Steerage passengers, Ch. Telfer, that his chest had been tampered with, and had been forced with a blunt chisel, or something, I accordingly by order of Captn. Hoyle searched the accused F. Ross and found on his person a gold pencil which was claimed by Robt. Drysdale, steerage passenger, as being his property and was taken from the bag along with the money and

---

[14]Henry Charles Moore Almon is listed in the Agreement and Account of Crew for this voyage as an apprentice. Apparently he had been promoted by this date. He was 19. Including Almon, there were four apprentices signed aboard at the start of the voyage, two of whom left the ship at Napier, N.Z. Almon returned to England in the *Euterpe.*

checque or draft for £30 that was stolen last week. When searching his effects I found four plugs or part plugs of tobacco that he could not account for satisfactorily, also numerous knives, one of which was claimed by Thos. Whally asst. Cook, three books and three sheets, three towels, three pillow slips, all of which were claimed by Mr. Galloway, cabin passenger, also one sheet and three towels claimed by Mr. Orr, cabin passgr., as his property. . . .

The accused denied all knowledge of stealing the articles, saying they all belonged to himself. I also found by his books and papers that he was travelling under an assumed name, his name being Frank De Rhodes, or Frank Ross de Rhodes.

The accused after a few hours reflection, acknowledged having taken the Gold pencil from Mr. Drysdale's bag, the tobacco from various parties, the pillow slips and towels and books from Mr. Galloway and Brown's cabin and Mr. Orr's cabin, but he denied all knowledge of the draft or the £9.

At 8 P.M. F. Ross De Rhodes after telling repeated falsehoods said he had something that he would like to tell to the Captain, that he intended to tell the truth and be done with it. So before Capn. Hoyle and I, he accused Charles Telfor, steerage passenger, with having been tampering with Drysdale's bag, he having seen Telfor through the cracks in the partition that seperated the storeroom from the single men's berth, he being in the store room at the time along with the passenger steward James Auld. He said this occured on Sunday 27th April, in the afternoon. He said he saw Telfor opening the bag and abstracting the pocket book. He said he never let on to any one about this until last Wednesday or Thursday, he happening to be in the berth saw some tobacco in Mr. Allan's bed which he took not thinking that any one could see him but next day Mr. Telfor accused him with stealing the tobacco, and told him that he would inform the Captain on him. He said that he retaliated on Telfor and accused him with stealing Drysdale's money. Telfor, he said, then asked him to keep quiet, and so would he, and promised him £5 when he got the draft cashed. He said he asked Telfor how much was in the purse and Telfor told him only £3 and the draft and two letters.

I immediately by orders of Capn. Hoyle searched Telfor and all his effects but could find no trace of any property belonging to any one. Ross or De Rhodes swore to this statement on Bible oath before & after I searched Mr. Telfor.

Tuesday 6th May
Frank Ross De Rhodes this day before Capn. Hoyle, Mr. Allan, Mr. Drysdale, & W. Paterson, acknowledged having abstracted the pocket book, and the money he kept, the letters and pocketbook he threw overboard. He also said that all his previous declaration was false and Telfor had nothing to do with abstracting the pocket book. Mr. Telfor was according[ly] called into the cabin and his character cleared before everyone. Ross or De Rhodes signed papers acknowledging all his misdeeds.

Captain Hoyle's Log
Tuesday, 6th
Spoke Barque "Kooringa", late "Ravonstondale", 13 days out from Liverpool for Valparaiso. . . .

Mr. Paterson's Log
Wednesday 7th May 84
Brisk breeze & fine clear weather. Crew overhauling blocks Fore Main & miz. . . .
Carpenter wedging miz. lower cap and renewing cleets etc.

Thursday 8th May 84
Brisk trade wind and fine clear weather continues. . . .
Carpenter fitting up wood racks in fore hold etc. Crew variously employed at blocks and overhauling foot ropes on the fore & lower yards.
Ship "San Stephano" on our weather qrtr.
Noon. Steady breeze, clear atmosphere. All sail set.
Dist. per Log, 157 Miles.

Friday 9th May 84
Commences with the wind gradually veering Easterly. Cloudy

& overcast during the afternoon.

Making a main deck awning out of old upper topsail.[15]

Saturday 10th May 84

Painting oil room & fixing all oils in position. Making awning for quarter deck etc. . . .

Carpenter oiling yards, wheel gear and all iron work requiring oil. Crew overhauling main foot ropes and main lower topsail foot ropes. . . .

Sighting through his sextant, a skipper begins to calculate his position. In the *Euterpe,* both Captain Hoyle and Mate William Paterson performed this procedure daily, weather permitting.

---

[15]A sure sign of the equator's approach. The ship this day reached 9°31′ N, 24°41′ W.

Sunday 11th May 84

. . . A moderate & steady breeze from the N.E. continues, all drawing sail set throughout.

No work doing this day Sunday after washing down.

Monday 12th May 84

6 P.M. Threatening appearance ahead with vivid flashes of lightning.

7 P.M. Wind veered south in a sharp squall accompanied with heavy rain, stowed royals & small staysails.

Midnight.[16] Light westerly airs & fine clear weather. All sail set. . . .

Tuesday 13th May 84

. . . 3.30 P.M. Heavy bank to the S.E. Stowed royals and all small sails.

4 to 6. Heavy rain wind light from the SE then variable.

9 P.M. . . . Wind & weather very unsettled. . . .

Noon. Very light SE breeze with warm oppresive weather. Dist. per Log, 47 Miles.[17]

Wednesday 14th May 84

. . . 4 A.M. Tacked ship to SW.

4 to 8. Variable airs and showery at intervals.

Carpenter repairing rails on the poop. Crew making service and standing by. . . .

Thursday 15th May 84

. . . 1.20 A.M. Calm, Calm.

4 A.M. Squally with heavy rain from the SW. . . .

Friday 16th May 84

Commences with a very light air. At 1.30 a sharp squall accompanied with rain, which continues to 4 P.M. . . .

---

[16]I.e., midnight of the 11th, as this entry was made at noon of the 12th.

[17]Down from 142 miles two days earlier. *Euterpe* was in the Doldrums.

Saturday 17th May 84

Noon. Wind fell off to a Calm which continues up to 6 P.M. Boxhauling yards round in all directions, 6 P.M. a very light SE breeze. . . .

A.M. Wind veering southerly gradually freshening.

Carpenter at battens oiling etc., etc. Crew at various jobs aloft serving jib pendants etc.

Signalized the Barq "Kooringa" again, exchanged & compared time by chrontr. . . .[18]

B. Johnsen A.B. laid up sick with Venereal disease.

Sunday 18th May 84

. . . No work started after washing decks this day, Sunday.

Noon. Brisk & steady SE breeze & fine clear wr.

B. Johnsen A.B. laid up sick (Venereal disease).

Lat. by Ob. 1°4′ South 29 Days out.[19]

Monday 19th May 84

P.M. commences with a brisk steady SE trade wind & fine clear weather all sail set.

Overhauling the "Kooringa" fast, also another vessel right ahead. . . .

Carpenter caulking poop deck. Crew repairing chafes, cleared out lower fore peak and got the sluce [sic] valve in working order.

Signalized the Barq "Helena" a German from Melbourne to Falmouth.[20]

B. Johnsen at his work again.

---

[18]I.e., by chronometer. John G. Rogers, in *Origins of Sea Terms*, defines its use: "A highly accurate clock used in navigation, which also served as a ship's master clock. While in use . . . some time earlier, it was not highly enough developed to be considered dependable until the mid-XIX century."

[19]During the night of the 17th/18th, the ship crossed the equator at about 27°W, not far east of the St. Paul Rocks.

[20]The *Helena's* route indicates she'd recently rounded Cape Horn from west to east.

Tuesday 20th May 84

. . . A.M. Wind gradually falling off to almost Calm towards 4 A.M. Wind very unsteady throughout. . . .

Crew repairing chafes aloft and various other needful jobs about.

Noon. Light airs and passing squalls and then *Calm*.

Wednesday 21st May 84

. . . 6 to 8 P.M. Strong breeze with hard squalls and rain, handed Miz & Fore royals & small stay sails. . . .

1 A.M. Weather clearing wind moderating set all sail.

3.45 Passed a Barque bound North. . . .

Thursday 22nd May 84

. . . Started the condenser in the morning for a trial and made 200 Galls of fresh water found everything in good working order. . . .

Carpenter making battens for rigging and other sundry small jobs. . . . Crew at various jobs aloft and fixing rolling tackles on the lower yards.

Noon. Very light unsteady Trades.

Friday 23rd May 84

Commences with light unsteady breeze from the SE weather looking very unsettled.

7 P.M. Drizling rain wind veering to Sthrd. . . .

A.M. Moderate breeze with fine clear weather all sail set.

Carpenter making battens & caulking forecastle upper deck. Crew repairing outer jib sheets & renewing pendants, painted bowsprit & figure head, etc. . . .[21]

B. Johnsen A.B. laid up sick (Venereal disease).

---

[21]The ship's figurehead, a portrait of the muse Euterpe, was carved by George Sutherland of Glasgow in 1863. Although damaged in collisions, most of the original sculpture survives.

Captain Hoyle's Log
Saturday, 24th
Through the night strong SE wind and hard squalls of wind and rain with very high SE sea—vessel diving bows under continually and flooding decks.

Noon: Moderate gale and fine: top gallant sails in—passed a barque under lower topsails—also two vessels standing Eastward.

4 P.M.: Wore ship to the Eastward: Strong wind and hard gusts with high sea.

Week's run 1001 miles.

Mr. Paterson's Log
Saturday 24th May 84
P.M. Begins with a moderate SSE breeze and very fair weather. Painting head gear.

7 P.M. A sharp squall from the Sthrd. with a heavy shower of rain.

9 P.M. Wind freshening with a heavy Sthrd. sea.

10 P.M. Wind and sea increasing, handed Miz & Fore top gallant sails spanker and all small sails.

A.M. Heavy head sea shipping large quantities of water over the bow, heavy squalls at intervals with rain. Crew standing by, weather too boisterous to start any jobs. Passed one Vessel bound NE and one bound to Sthrd.

Noon. Strong breeze with short choppy sea, ship pitching heavily.

B. Johnsen started work again.

Captain Hoyle's Log
Sunday, 25th
2 A.M. Wore ship to the SW. . . .

8 P.M. . . very squally with rain & high head sea. . . .

Passed Steamer "Laplace" bound for Dunkirk and asked him to report us all well. Passed a barque on S. Tack.

Mr. Paterson's Log
     Sunday 25th May 84
     Begins with a strong breeze and head sea, ship diving heavy.
     1.30 P.M. Handed Main Tgt. sail.
     4 P.M. Wore Ship to the Eastrd. Shipping large quantities of
water over the bow. . . .
     At 1.30 A.M. Wore Ship to the Sthrd., and set main Tgt. sail.
     4 A.M. Moderate breeze from the ESE head sea going down
set outer job & Fore topgt. sail. . . .
     6.30 Set all sail weather clearing.
     8 Signalized S.S. "Laplace" bound to Dunkerque. . . .

"6.30 Set all sail weather clearing." One of the sailor's many arduous tasks was
going aloft in all weathers to set, reef, or furl sail. In this modern photo,
volunteers climb the ship's port shrouds to the main top. Behind them, others
lay out on the main yard.

SAN DIEGO MARITIME MUSEUM FILE PHOTO

Monday 26th May 84

P.M. Commences with a moderate SE breeze and fair weather. . . .

5.30 Sharp squalls handed royals & small staysails. . . .

A.M. Sharp squalls at intervals.

3.30 Weather clearing set the three topgallansails & spanker. . . .

Captain Hoyle's Log

Tuesday, 27th

8 A.M. Light ESE wind and fine. . . .

Passed Steamer "Tongariro" steering Northward — he gave us Longitude at 9 A.M.

Mr. Paterson's Log

Tuesday 27th May 84

. . . 5 A.M. Weather clear & fine made all sail.

Carpenter at leads for gear & battens and sundry other jobs. Crew renewing ratlines Fore Main & Mz.

9 A.M. Passed the S.S. "Tongariro" from New Zealand bound North. . . .

Wednesday 28th May 84

Commences with a light SE and fair weather, light showers occasionally. . . .

Carpenter caulking forecastle head. Crew repairing ratlines etc. etc. . . .

Thursday 29th May 84

. . . 3.30 A.M. Wind veering to Norrd. brisk, sky overcast. . . .

---

[22]This entry and one on the 31st makes it evident the men were preparing for the Roaring Forties. The ship was riding the Brazil Current southward, each day bringing her about one degree in latitude closer to where the westerlies blew. For those winds, they would need the "nun's shift" aloft — the ship's stoutest, most unyielding canvas.

Crew setting up all the head gear and Fore topmast Topgt. & Royal backstays. . . .
Dist. per Log, 195 Miles.

Friday 30th May 84
. . . 5 P.M. A heavy downpour of rain, wind unsteady . . . .
Weather cleared, wind light, all drawing sail set. . . .
8 A.M. Crew bending best sails. . . .[22]

Captain Hoyle's Log
Saturday, 31st
Noon: Light NE breeze and very fine with high NE swell.
8 P.M. Light Northerly breeze and very fine; halo round the moon.
Week's run 671.

Mr. Paterson's Log
Saturday 31st May 84
P.M. Very light breeze almost a calm, all hands employed bending heavy weather sails. . . .
Carpenter making cabin port tight etc., oiling fore & aft also. Crew bending royals & Miz. S.S. overhauling topsail buntlines bending all gear. . . .

[June 1884: This month saw the *Euterpe* stand away toward the Cape of Good Hope (more aptly known as the "Cape of Storms" by sailors). She bowled down into the Roaring Forties — that belt of wild westerly winds in the latitudes from 40°South to 50°South, approximately. These winds would blow her all the way to New Zealand — but not without a price. Death, injuries, and many days of parlous sailing lay ahead. Beginning in this month, we print only excerpts from her more eventful days, passing over much of the routine detailed during the first two months of the voyage.]

Captain Hoyle's Log
Monday, 2nd
Strong Southerly wind and gusty with fine weather and high sea. Auld, Steward, fell and severely hurt himself.

Mr. Paterson's Log
Monday 2nd June 84
. . . 2 A.M. Handed Miz topgt sail Miz topmast staysail main topgallant staysail. Wind coming in fitfull gusts.
6 to 8. Sea rising wind very unsteady weather clear.
Carpenter at a box for Standard compass. Crew at spar lashings and all boats & loose gear. . . .
Lat. by Ob. 25°26′ South. Lon. by Ob. 31°42′ W.[23]

Tuesday 3rd June 84
. . . A.M. Wind & weather very unsettled, ship rolling very heavy, straining everything.
Washed in the steerage passengers w.c. Carpenter caulking and battening after hatch, cleeted & secured it thoroughly. Crew making mats for yards etc.
Noon. Brisk breeze with heavy beam sea.

Captain Hoyle's Log
Friday, 6th
1st Albatross seen.

Saturday, 7th
1st Cape Pigeon seen. Week's run 848 miles.

Mr. Paterson's Log
Tuesday 10th June 84
. . . 6 A.M. Wind veered NE with fine wr. Carpenter caulking forecastle deck. Crew repairing chafes sent down the fore topgallant tye renewed shackles and fixed crosstree legs etc. Forrd. . . .

---

[23]I.e., the ship had crossed the Tropic of Capricorn and was about 800 miles east of Rio de Janeiro. Her course was now southeast.

Wednesday 11th June 84

P.M. . . . Unshipped main deck capstan, scraped and painted it. . . .

12 to 4 A.M. A strong breeze with slight showers.

2 A.M. Wind veered NW all fore and aft canvas furled.

Carpenter finished caulking Forecastle head. Sent down Main topsail tie and cut out a damaged link renewed shackles etc. & overhauled gins etc. . . .

Captain Hoyle's Log

Thursday, 12th

6 A.M. Wind shifted to the Westward with heavy rain afterwards sharp WNW wind and cloudy weather.

8 P.M. Fresh WSW gale and very gusty: vessel shipping much water at times.

Mr. Paterson's Log

Thursday 12th June 84

. . . Midnight. Wind continues Strong sea rising shipping a few seas on the deck.

A.M. Strong breeze continues ship running very easy. . . .

Friday 13th June 84

Strong & increasing breeze with passing squalls sea rising & shipping large quantities of water on the deck.

8 P.M. Moderate Gale with heavy squalls, handed royals & Miz topgallant sail & crossjack.

Midnight. Breeze moderating heavy westerly sea, running before it, ship running very dry.

Sunday 15th June 84

P.M. Commences with light baffling airs & almost calm at times lee clews of Courses hauled up everything banging about and geting knocked to pieces. . . .

A.M. Light airs continues Nasty sea Ship rolling about in all directions. . . .

Monday 16th June 84

P.M. Light breeze from ENE gradually freshening nasty cross sea ship labouring heavily all sail now set. . . .

Wednesday 18th June 84

. . . 3 P.M. Moderate Gale stowed Miz & Fore royals & crossjack.

6.45 Wind veering to Westrd Brisk Gale handed main royal. . . .

Captain Hoyle's Log

Friday, 20th

Fresh wind through the night backing round from the Westward to NW and NNW to North with thick rain — increasing at 5 A.M. to fresh gale with hard gusts.

At 6 A.M.: freshening rapidly called all hands and reduced sail to upper topsails wind shifting to WNW with heavy rain . . . blowing fresh gale at 8 A.M. with sky overcast.

Noon: Heavy gale W by N and hard squalls with high sea — shipping much water at times. Vessel under lower mizen topsail — whole fore & main topsails & Foresail.

8 P.M. Fresh W by S to West wind and very squally with rain and high sea.

Mr. Paterson's Log

Friday 20th June 84

. . . Midnight. Passing showers wind aft Ship rolling heavily. . . .

4 A.M. Heavy rain falling Bartr. handed topgallantsails & crossjack.

5 Called all hands furled mainsail & miz topsail & main tgt. sail.

5.30 A very heavy squall wind Hurricane force with torrents of rain lowered the topsails.

6 Wind veered West Strong Gale. Ship labouring heavily & shipping large quantities of water.

Noon. Strong Westerly Gale heavy sea.

Captain Hoyle's Log
Saturday, 21st
Fresh westerly gale throughout the night with hail squalls towards daylight. . . .

At Noon: Fresh WSW wind and squally with rain. Strong WSW gale throughout the afternoon and sharp squalls of hail and wind.

8 P.M. Strong SW gale—hard squalls and high sea—lightning to the Eastward.

Mr. Paterson's Log
Saturday 21st June 84
Strong Westerly Gale and heavy sea Shipping large quantities of water on the deck, Ship labouring and straining everything.

3 P.M. Gale moderating set mizen topsail & main topgt. sail. . . .

Crew mat & service making, fitted Foretopmast staysail sheet whips.

Noon. Passing hail squalls, Moderate Gale.

Sunday 22nd June 84
. . . Midnight. Heavy hail squalls occasionally, Brisk Gale. Shipping large quantities of water on the deck.

A.M. Heavy squalls continue throughout the watch. Ship labouring and Shipping large volumes of water. . . .

Monday 23rd June 84
. . . A.M. Wind very unsteady beam sea making up, faint Lightning ahead & astern Ship lurching heavily.

7 A.M. Wind veered SW with drizling rain.
8 Moderate breeze ship rolling heavy straining everything.
10 Made sail, weather clearing.
Noon. Brisk breeze all sail set.

Tuesday 24th June 84
. . . 3 A.M. Wind freshening to a Gale stowed Main topgt. sail.
4 A.M. Gale increasing stowed Jib & Miz upper topsail.

6 A.M. Fresh Gale & dirty looking Weather. Ship running very steady & dry. . . .

Crew renewing rovings unbent & repaired Fore top-gallant sail, rove Fore topgt. buntlines new 2¼ Europe.[24]

Noon. Strong gale & dirty weather.

Captain Hoyle's Log
Wednesday, 25th
. . . throughout the afternoon light Southerly airs and thick misty weather with a confused swell . . . vessel rolling and labouring heavily and flooding decks. . . .

Mr. Paterson's Log
Wednesday 25th June 84
Commences with a Strong Gale with thick murky weather, sea making up aft. . . .

6.30 A.M. Wind fell away with thick drizling rain. . . .
Boxhauling yards about in all directions, Ship drifting about.

Captain Hoyle's Log
Thursday, 26th
J. Campbell stowaway whilst overhauling topgallant buntlines fell from aloft to the deck breaking both legs and otherwise severely injuring himself—put both legs in splints and did everything possible for him—the right leg terribly smashed and bones all in pieces and much flesh torn away from the leg.

Mr. Paterson's Log
Thursday 26th June 84
Commences with very light variable airs, and heavy cross sea. Ship rolling very much & straining everything Shipping large quantities of water on the deck. Courses & topgallantsail clewed up all Fore & aft canvas fast. . . .

6 A.M. Bent Fore topgallantsail Carpenter blockmaking etc. opened main & after hatches found every thing secure sealed them up again secure.

---

[24]"Europe" was a type of line, like "Manilla."

Noon. All available sail set weather clear & fine.

At 11 A.M. John Campbell stowaway having been sent aloft to the main royal yard to clear the gear, lost his hold and came down from aloft striking various things on the way down, breaking both legs and otherwise injuring himself.

Captain Hoyle's Log
Friday, 27th
Campbell still unconscious and raving considerably—managed to take some arrowroot both last night and this morning—one hand constantly in attendance on him.

Mr. Paterson's Log
Friday 27th June 84
. . . 8 A.M. Very heavy squalls with sleet & rain, Thunder & Lightning hauled down main & miz stay sails & furled Fore topsail. . . .

John Campbell in a low condition not having recovered consciousness, everything possable done for him.

Captain Hoyle's Log
Saturday, 28th
Wind light and baffling through the first part from the Westward hauling suddenly to SE at 6 A.M. and increasing to fresh gale at noon—reefed topsails & set them. Fresh SE gale throughout the day with high sea and gloomy weather.

Campbell still unconscious and much quieter—took beef tea and was able to drink it—very little fever and rather cold at extremities.

Mr. Paterson's Log
Saturday 28th June 84
Commences with a Brisk Gale moderating to Strong breeze, head sea. . . .

At 5 A.M. Wind suddenly chopped to SE Strong handed Topgallantsails. . . .

Noon. Reefed topsails, Gale increasing, heavy squalls.
John Campbell still very low and unconscious.

Sunday 29th June 84
. . . Midnight. Gale continues Strong weather clearing at times
shipping large quantities of water over the bow. . . .
7 A.M. Wind inclined to veer to Sthrd. weather dull & overcast. . . .
At 11.30 P.M. John Campbell passed away very quiet.
8 A.M. Mustered all hands aft. Capn. Hoyle performed the
burial service, & commited the body to the deep.

Monday 30th June 84
Commences with a Brisk Gale clear at intervals . . . .
9 P.M. Shook reef out Fore topsail. Shipped a very heavy sea
over the bows, but did no perceptable damage . . . .
6 A.M. Squalls moderating set Miz topsail & Jib.
Carpenter puting up 2 bunks in forecastle, others leaking.

[July 1884: *Euterpe* had passed the longitude of the Cape of
Good Hope on June 22nd, and by July 1st she was
running eastward through the Roaring Forties in a
turbulent zone bordered by the Indian Ocean to the
north and the forbidding Southern Ocean to the
south. Icebergs — the huge, tabular Antarctic type —
now made their appearances, along with plummeting
temperatures. (July, of course, is the middle of winter
in those latitudes.) On the 17th, when the ship was
in the Southern Ocean 1200 miles south of the Great
Australian Bight, a near-disastrous storm of "hurricane force" struck, building to its height by the 20th.
Many ships went missing with all hands in these
desolate seas, but the *Euterpe* struggled on. Frequently the winds blew her more than 200 sea miles per
day. Death continued to stalk the ship, along with
sickness and some serious damage to her rigging. Yet
this was the final leg to New Zealand, and the end

of the month would bring our weary vessel within sight of its shores.]

Captain Hoyle's Log
Tuesday, 1st
Noon: Moderate SW to SSW wind and cloudy. Southerly & SW swell. . . .
Lat. 42°57' S. Long. 50°41' E.

Wednesday, 2nd
Passed a large Iceberg—at 11 A.M. to the Northward about 5 miles. . . .

Thursday, 3rd
Passed a large Iceberg at 4 P.M. to the Northwest—distant about 8 to 10 miles. . . .

A captain's life wasn't all work. There were days to relax a bit on deck and perhaps enjoy a pipe. Here a skipper of the period takes his ease on one of the milder days.

Mr. Paterson's Log
Friday 4th July 84
Commences with moderate breeze and fine clear weather. SW
swell making up. . . . A large iceberg to the Norrd. . . .
Carpenter repairing blocks and packing rudder underneath
cabin. Crew overhauling luff tackle & purchase blocks cleaning
& painting them etc. . . .

Captain Hoyle's Log
Saturday, 5th
Week's run 1174 miles. . . .

Sunday, 6th
Fresh gale through the night with rain & sleet veering gradually
to E by S. . . . At 8 A.M. wore ship to the Southward.
Noon: Moderate gale Easterly & thick rain. . . .

Mr. Paterson's Log
Tuesday 8th July 84
. . . Weather clear up to 7 A.M. then misty showers. Fresh
breeze. . . .
10 A.M. Wind backing to Norrd. very unsteady.
11 A.M. Heavy rain. Wind chopped suddenly into SW. Heavy
NW swell Ship labouring & straining.

Captain Hoyle's Log
Wednesday, 9th
Much Kelp. Fresh Southerly to SSE gale throughout the night
with clear weather; at 8 A.M. more moderate — set M.T.G. sail. . . .

Mr. Paterson's Log
Thursday 10th July 84
Commences with a brisk SE breeze gradually moderating com-
ing away in gusts, weather clearing, set Fore & Main topgtsls.
3.30 Wind veering East, Wore Ship to Sthrd. . . .
Bent the new Foresail sent the 2nd one down for repairs.

Carpenter repairing blocks & shieves. Crew mat making repairing U.M. topsail. . . .

Captain Hoyle's Log
Tuesday, 15th
Variable airs mostly SE to Easterly throughout the night hauling yards round several times. . . . high Southerly swell.
Kelp — Also passed some wreckage apparently a spar with sail attached.

Thursday, 17th
Moderate WNW wind throughout the night increasing at 8 A.M. to hard gale with sharp squalls continuing same weather at Noon: vessel under topsails & foresail.
Fresh WNW gale through the afternoon increasing at 4 P.M. to hard gale NW by N in a fierce squall of hail and wind.
Lightning to the Eastward and strong gale at 8 P.M. at W by N and long regular sea. Vessel under whole main topsails and fore upper topsail fast. Vessel running very dry.
Carried away S. Main T.G. sheet at 10.30 A.M.

Mr. Paterson's Log
Thursday 17th July 84
. . . 8 P.M. Stowed Mainsail & x jack. Wind aft, & appearance changeable.
9 P.M. Wind backed to WNW. Stowed main royal. . . .
8 A.M. Wind freshening suddenly to gale handed royals x jack & miz. topgt. sail.
9 Stowed Fore topgt. sail.
11 Maintopgt. sheet whip carried away furled the sail.
Noon. Furled mainsail. . . .

Friday 18th July 84
. . . 3 P.M. Very threatening appearance towards the SW.
3.30 A terrific hail squall furled fore topsail and squared the yards running before a Strong Gale.
8 P.M. Vivid flashes of lightning from all quarters. . . .

Midnight. Strong steady gale. . . .

8.30 A.M. Gale increasing backing to WNW . . . reefed Fore & Main topsails. Strong gale sea rising sun obscure.

Captain Hoyle's Log
Friday, 18th
. . . Noon: Increasing WNW gale and squally with high sea from WNW to WSW: reefed topsails.

At 4 P.M. wind shifted to West in a hard squall with sleet and at 7 P.M. rapidly increased to heavy gale and furious squalls with a mountainous sea rising. At 10 P.M. wind veering to W by S with hard squalls. At 11 P.M. filled up main deck to the rails and much water getting below. At 11.30 more moderate — set whole main topsail.

Midnight: Moderate W by S gale & gusty with a mountainous sea.

Mr. Paterson's Log
Saturday 19th July 84
Very strong gale from WNW with a very heavy sea furled Main Upper topsail.

4 P.M. Wind suddenly veered to WSW in a terrific hail squall. . . .

8 P.M. Shipping large volumes of water on the deck. Very heavy sea. . . . Frequent heavy hail squalls.

10 Weather clearing set main topsail, shipping large volumes of water on the deck filling up the main deck completely, a quantity penetrating the afterhatch also the cabin. . . .

8 A.M. to Noon. Frequent Squalls hail & snow. . . .

Sunday 20th July 84
P.M. Brisk Gale with frequent squalls up to 2 P.M. weather cleared gale abating set main topgsl. . . .

7 P.M. Wind veering Westerly set main royal ship labouring heavily. . . .

Midnight. Banking up on Port quarter furled main royal strong breeze. . . .

2.30 A.M. Wind freshening to a Gale stowed Main topgt. sail.

3.30 Fresh Gale stowed Miz. topsail.

4 A.M. Strong Gale reefed & stowed Fore & Main topsails.

7 A.M. Gale increasing to violent force stowed miz. lower topsail.

7.15 A most terrific Hail Squall wind Hurricane force from WNW to WSW.

9.30 Gale continues most Violent sea rising to dangerous height hauled up Foresail & brought the Ship to the Wind. As the Ship came to, the foot rope of Fore Topsail carried away bursting sail from clew to earing, tack of Foretopmast staysail also carried away and damaged the head rails hauling sail down. Set tarpaulin in Miz. rigging to keep Ship to, clew of Miz. staysail having burst.

11 Set Main topmast staysail to steady the Ship.

Noon. Gale blowing with unabated force. Ship lying to very steady in a most mountainous sea.

Captain Hoyle's Log

Sunday, 20th

Wind backed to WNW at midnight and began increasing rapidly with rain and at 4 A.M. reduced sail to lower topsails & Foresail.

At 8 A.M. terrific squall of wind & hail — wind veering to West and at 10 A.M. blowing heavy gale with terrific squalls of hail with a mountainous sea rising. Hove ship to on the Port tack under two lower topsails. Shortly after coming to the wind lower fore topsail blew away also tack cringle of Fore topmast staysail parted — blowing a heavy gale at W by S till 3 P.M. when it began to moderate.

Bent best lower fore topsail & kept ship away at 4 P.M. NE by E½E & set upper main topsail. Weather still unsettled and high Westerly sea running. . . .

At 8 P.M.: Moderate gale WSW to W by S and squally.

Mr. Paterson's Log
    Monday 21st July 84
    P.M. Lying to under lower main topsail Main & Miz. staysail & weather cloth, a most mountainous sea. Shipping large quantities of water over lee rail.
    3 P.M. Unbent Fore lower topsl and at 4 bent a new one. Gale abating fast.
    At 5 Squared away set Foresail lower topsails & main upper topsail.
    8 to Midnight. Brisk Gale to a strong breeze weather very unsettled-looking bartr. low. Hail & sleet squalls at intervals sea going down fast. . . .
    Hail & sleet squalls continue at intervals up to 7 A.M. when weather cleared. Set sail according.
    Carpenter at various jobs Fore & aft. Crew repairing sails etc., rove new Force brace on Port side. . . .
    Reid sick off duty. Duff sick off duty.

Captian Hoyle's Log
    Tuesday, 22nd
    Weather unsettled throughout the night with wind unsteady between W by N and WSW and squally with snow and hail. . . .
    Mr. Orr very unwell and delirious.[25]

    Wednesday, 23rd
    Fresh WNW to NW wind through the night freshening during the forenoon with light rain. Topgallant sails—mainsail & crossjack in at noon with Strong NW wind and overcast and sea rising. Gale steadily increasing and at 8 P.M. vessel under reefed topsails. At Midnight—hard gale with thick rain—wind NW by W to WNW.
    Mr. Orr still unconscious but taking nourishment.

---

[25]Francis Orr was one of the cabin passengers involved in the Frank Ross de Rhodes theft incidents in early May.

Thursday, 24th
Heavy gale WNW and high sea with thick rain. At 3 A.M. shipped a heavy sea over the poop breaking down rail aft—putting much water in the cabin and washing all movables overboard— smashed in galley door and sundry other damage. . . .

At Noon moderate westerly gale and high sea with squally weather—vessel shipping much water on deck. Weather very unsettled during the afternoon with squalls and a mountainous westerly swell. . . .

Mr. Orr rather better and able to converse.

Mr. Paterson's Log
Thursday 24th July 84
Commences with a Brisk & freshening Gale, reefed the Top-sails. . .

6 P.M. Very heavy squalls furled Fore & Miz topsails & jib. Sea rising with crested tops. . . .

2 A.M. Gale freshening stowed Miz lower topsail, Pooped a heavy sea smashing in the poop rail on port quarter, also burst the screens, burst galley door and wash away pipe casing.

7 A.M. Weather clearing wind moderating set Miz lower top reefed Fore topsails. Carpenter repairing damage with crews assistance.

Noon Brisk Gale. Reef out main topsail.

Friday 25th July 84
P.M. Brisk Gale heavy NW sea Ship labouring & shipping much water on deck at times. . . .

Midnight. Heavy sleet squalls furled main topgt. sail.

A.M. Brisk Gale with heavy Hail & sleet squalls throughout. Wind veering WSW.

8 A.M. Squalls continues at intervals clearing a little towards 8 A.M. Carpenter blocking up ports in cabin some having got cracked & broken with the sea.

Noon. Fresh Gale with sea making up from SW passing squalls.

SANCTIONED BY THE BOARD OF
TRADE, MAY 1855.
IN PURSUANCE OF 17 & 18 VICT. c. 104.

(O)

OFFICIAL LOG BOOK No. 4.

FOR

EITHER FOREIGN-GOING OR HOME TRADE SHIP.

Name of Ship.	Official Number.	Port of Registry.	Registered Tonnage.	Name of Master.	No. of his Certificate (if any).
"Euterpe"	47617	London	1197	William Cowen	13567

Date of Commencement of the Voyage _August 31st 1869_

Nature of the Voyage or Employment _London to Bombay Rangoon and_

Delivered to the Shipping Master of the Port of _London Poplar_ the _10th_

day of _October_ 18 _70._

Signed _________________
Shipping Master.

NOTE.—The above Entries are to be filled up by the Master, and the Log Book is to be delivered to the Shipping Master within forty-eight hours after the Ship's arrival, or upon the discharge of the Crew, whichever first happens, in the case of a "Foreign-going Ship;" and within twenty-one days after the 30th of June and the 31st of December respectively in every year in the case of a "Home Trade Ship."—*See* 286.

LONDON:
PRINTED BY GEORGE EDWARD EYRE AND WILLIAM SPOTTISWOODE,
PRINTERS TO THE QUEEN'S MOST EXCELLENT MAJESTY.
1867.

The front page of one of *Euterpe's* logs, this one dating from 1869-70. Among other details, it gives the ship's port of registry, tonnage (1197) and route (London to Bombay and Rangoon).

SOURCE: NATIONAL MARITIME MUSEUM, LONDON, U.K.

Captain Hoyle's Log
     Friday, 25th
Gale freshened at W by S to WSW with frequent hard squalls
and a very high sea. At noon Moderate gale and hard squalls with
high sea. Heavy gale WSW to SW through the afternoon with
fierce squalls of hail and sleet.
     Mr. Orr remaining in about same condition.
     8 P.M. Heavy SW gale with continuous hail squalls and sleet
with a mountainous WSW sea. Continuing same weather to midnight with dangerous sea.

Mr. Paterson's Log
     Saturday 26th July 84
Fresh Gale with heavy hail & sleet squalls throughout. . . .
Ship labouring & shipping water all over fore & aft.
     Midnight. Gale abating sea going down wind veering
sthrly. . . .
     9.30 A.M. Mr. Francis D. Orr cabin passenger died, cause
dropsy.[26]

     Sunday 27th July 84
P.M. Brisk Sthrly Gale with rising sea, Heavy SW swell Hail
& sleet squalls.
     1.30 Buried Mr. Orr, Capn Hoyle reading service in Cabin.
     8 P.M. Wind moderating & sea going down. . . .
     5 A.M. Wind falling light. Made all sail towards 8 A.M.

Captain Hoyle's Log
     Monday, 28th
Hard SSW gale and heavy squalls with a high sea — vessel
under lower topsails — foresail & staysails.
     Noon: more moderate: set reefed topsails — fresh S by W to
SSW gale and squally with high sea — washed away part of top
gallant bulwarks: — starboard side amidships.

---

[26]Dropsy is characterized by retention of fluids with possible uremic poison-
ing, and ultimately by failure of the heart or kidneys.

Mr. Paterson's Log
Monday 28th July 84

Commences with a moderate breeze backing gradually to westrd. and freshening all fore & aft canvas fast, x jack & mainsail.

8 P.M. Squally royals & fore & miz topgt. sails fast.

9 P.M. Freshening to Gale stowed main topgt. miz & fore topsails.

Midnight. Fresh Gale.

1 A.M. Very violent squalls stowed main topsail.

3 A.M. Strong Gale.

6 A.M. Hail & Sleet squalls continue very violent set reefed main topsail & Fore topsail.

Noon. Fresh Gale with hail & sleet squalls heavy sea ship labouring & shipping large quantities of water.

100 Days out.

Captain Hoyle's Log
Tuesday, 29th

. . . At 8 P.M. wind increasing to heavy gale — westerly to WSW with hard squalls brought ship to the wind on the P. Tack under lower fore & main topsails. Taking casts of the lead frequently and at midnight got bottom at 75 fms. Wore ship to the southward.

47°53′ S. 168°20′ E.

Wednesday, 30th

Heavy WSW gale and terrific squalls of wind & hail — carried away mizen stay. At 6 A.M. rather more moderate. Kept ship away to North — at 7 A.M. rapidly increasing gale — brought ship to the wind on the P. Tack — taking several casts of the lead during the forenoon — no bottom — towards noon passed much seaweed and at noon got bottom at 55 fms — at same time sighted land to the Westward but could not distinguish it — wore ship to the Southward — shortly after getting ship round the crane of lower topsail yard (fore) gave way and yard came down — got it on deck and secured in P. Fore rigging and sail unbent. Blowing a terrific gale with hurricane squalls of hail & wind with mountainous sea. Vessel labouring heavily and shipping much water fore & aft. . . .

Mr. Paterson's Log

Tuesday 29th July 84

P.M. Brisk SSW Gale hail & sleet squalls. . . .

8 A.M. Moderate Gale from WSW.

Hove up chain cables bent them & secured the anchors in stoppers & lashings.

Noon. Moderate Gale.

Wednesday 30th July 84

. . . 6 P.M. Very Strong Gale furled main upper & miz lower topsails.

7 P.M. Hauled up Foresail & brought the Ship to the wind set the main & miz staysails shipping large quantities of water on the deck.

11.30 Sounded in 75 Fths. . . .

Midnight. Strong Gale with very heavy hail squalls wore Ship to SE.

3.30 Band of Miz stay carried away with force of wind in Miz stay sail.

6.30 Squared Yards & ran to Norrd for 40 minutes then brought Ship to P. tack. Wind increasing to a hurricane. Sounding at intervals no bottom at 80 fths.

Blowing a Hurricane with very heavy hail squalls at times. Wore Ship to SE having sighted the land.

Off Nugget Pt.[27] 102 Days out.

Thursday 31st July 84

Blowing a violent Hurricane with terrific Hail Squalls of long duration, at 1 P.M. the truss of lower Fore topsail yard carried away with the force of wind, yard coming down to leeward held by the sheets. With sail attached, secured the yard on deck with much difficulty and saved the Sail without much damage. Ship labouring heavily. Steady fall of rain with violent squalls Hail & sleet. Ship labouring in a most heavy mountainous sea.

4 A.M. Gale gradually moderating & sea going down fast.

---

[27]Nugget Point lies near the southeastern tip of South Island, New Zealand.

6 A.M. Squared Yards & stood to Norrd. then hauled up to wind & made for land.

9.30 A.M. Sighted land.

Noon. Cape Saunders bearing NW dist. about 25 Miles Ship have drifted about 30 with the Gale.

Noon. Made all available sail. Cape Saunders WNW dist. 20 Miles.

Friday 1st Aug. 84

Moderate breeze sea going down fast weather clear & fine.

2.30 P.M. Sighted Otago Heads but with strong tide setting to Norrd. was unable to fetch in.

5 P.M. Tacked Ship to Sthrd. Off land 4 miles. Taiaroa Pt. bearing SW by S, 18 miles. . . .

8.30 A.M. Pilot Mr. Millar boarded in pilot boat.

9 A.M. S.S. "Plucky" came alongside and Pilot Mr. Paton boarded and took charge furled all sail after giving tug the towrope.

Noon. Towing in toward the Heads. 104 days & finish off, Sea Log terminates.

Captain Hoyle's Log

Friday:—August 1

Moderate Westerly wind throughout the night working ship to the Southward—freshening at daylight. Recd. Pilot on board at 8 A.M. and about 10 A.M. tug Plucky took us in tow—furled all sail and came to anchor at 1 P.M. blowing a strong westerly wind & fine weather. At 10 P.M. came to anchor off Pt. Chalmers.

* * * * * *

"ARRIVAL OF THE EUTERPE"
[The *Otago Daily Times*, August 2nd, 1884]

The Shaw, Savill, and Albion Shipping Company's ship
Euterpe was towed into port yesterday evening by the s.s. Plucky,
and anchored off Deborah Bay at 10.30 p.m. Here she was met
by the Customs steam launch, and satisfactory answers having
been returned as to the health of passengers and crew, she was
promptly cleared in by Mr. MacDonnell, the tide-surveyor. The
members of the Press were cordially welcomed by the commander,
who willingly afforded them the necessary information as to the
passage out.

This is the earliest photograph extant of the ship under sail. Although she had
been rigged down to a barque by this date, the view of her from ahead with
the crew furling sail suggests how she might have looked on her approach to
a New Zealand port.

SAN DIEGO MARITIME MUSEUM FILE PHOTO

The Euterpe is a well-known trader to this port, and since her last visit here Captain Phillips, who then commanded her, has been transferred to the Zealandia, the command of the Euterpe devolving upon Captain Hoyle, who, although a stranger to this port, is an old visitant to New Zealand, his last vessel being the Merchant Shipping Company's ship Clyde, in which he successfully took immigrants last year to Auckland.

The Euterpe brings 1700 tons of cargo, of which two-thirds is dead weight; and has 28 passengers. The officers are—Mr. Paterson, chief; Mr. Wylie, second; Mr. Almon, third. We are indebted to Captain Hoyle for the following report of the passage out, which has occupied 104 days, and is decidedly the best she has yet made to this port:

She left Glasgow on April 9, but coming into collision with the s.s. Canadian, which carried away the ship's bowsprit and did other damage, she was compelled to return for repairs to Glasgow, and finally started on April 19; discharged her pilot off Waterford on the 22nd, and experienced variable winds, principally from the north-west, until she reached latitude 33 N., longitude 21 W., when she took the first of the N.E. trades, they were very light throughout, and gave out in latitude 5 N., longitude 23 W.

Thence she had variable airs and strong westerly currents down to latitude 1 N., longitude 26 W., where the S.E. trades commenced; they were well to the southward throughout, and hampered the ship very much all down the Brazilian coast, compelling her to make a tack to the eastward. The trades were lost in latitude 18 S., longitude 37 W., and were followed by baffling winds down to latitude 34 S., longitude 22 W., when the steady westerlies were taken, and she rounded the Cape of Good Hope in latitude 43 S., on the 63rd day out.

On June 26, in latitude 44 S., longitude 37 E., a melancholy accident occurred, by which a stowaway, a lad named J. Campbell, met his death. He fell from the maintopgallant masthead to the deck, breaking both legs and sustaining other severe injuries, which caused his death on the 29th June.

On July 2, in latitude 44 S., longitude 56 E., she passed a very large iceberg, and on the following day, in latitude 45 S., longitude

61 E., she passed another berg.

Very indifferent winds and weather prevailed from longitude 37 E. to longitude 110 E., and thence she encountered very heavy westerly gales; and on July 20 she met a hard gale with a mountainous sea, which broke on board and completely flooded the decks, causing the ship to heave to at 10 a.m. of that day, and shortly after she was rounded to, the lower foretopsail blew away. The gale moderated at 5 p.m., and the vessel was kept away.

Thence she had a continuance of heavy gales from W.N.W. to W.S.W., and on July 24, in latitude 48 S., longitude 152 E., a heavy sea broke over the port quarter, smashing the poop rail and doing other damage on deck, and flooding the cabin and steerage.

Hard S.W. gales were carried to abreast of the Snares, during which part of the starboard topgallant rails was washed away; and on July 30 a terrific W.S.W. gale set in at noon, and land was sighted to the westward. The gale then increased to hurricane force, and shortly after the vessel was wore round on the starboard tack the crane of the lower foretopsail yard gave away, and after great difficulty the yard was got on deck and properly secured. Heavy seas broke constantly over the ship, and on the 31st ult. the weather became more moderate, and she sighted Otago Heads at 10 a.m., but owing to the strong northerly current the ship was driven to the northward of the port; she took the pilot on board yesterday, and was towed up to the bar by the s.s. Plucky against a strong westerly wind, anchored until the evening, and was towed up as above.

We regret to mention that on July 26 Mr. F.D. Orr, a cabin passenger, died of dropsy, and was buried on the same day in latitude 45 S., longitude 157 E.

The s.s. Tongariro was passed, bound North, on May 27; since then no other vessels have been sighted. The easting was run down in the parallel of latitude of 48 S.

In reference to the death of the lad James Campbell by falling from the maintopgallant masthead of the ship Euterpe on June 26, our shipping reporter has interviewed Captain Hoyle, who distinctly avers the lad was never ordered aloft by him. The boy, however, was constantly aloft; and the captain adds that on the occasion of some athletic sports which were held on board the boy proved himself one of the most proficient of the competitors. He was one of three stowaways on board. The boy, to the best of Captain Hoyle's knowledge, went voluntarily aloft on June 26. He was in the act of overhauling the maintopgallant sail, while one of the ordinary seamen, Jones, was on the mizen. Campbell, it appears, waved his hands to Jones, and in doing so fell from the yard to the deck. Captain Hoyle's statement is borne out by that of Mr. Galloway, one of the passengers, who has repeatedly seen the deceased boy overhauling the ropes from the place from which he eventually fell. Upon close inquiry our reporter finds that the stowaways were well treated on board the Euterpe, and that nothing like "taking it out of him" seems to have been attempted by Captain Hoyle.

THE APPRENTICE'S LIFE

On the next page is a typical indenture of the late Victorian period. This one, dated May 1st, 1876, indentures one William Mullins, aged 15, of Limehouse in the eastern part of London, to one William Smith, Sailmaker, for a term of seven years. Smith resided at No. 8 Bow Lane, Poplar. Limehouse and Poplar are part of the East End's "Dockland" — both extending to the north of the old East India and West India docks. The Thames makes a great curve around the Isle of Dogs and flows down Blackwall Reach past these docks' entrances. On a number of her voyages, the *Euterpe* left the East India Docks, or returned there. This was truly the heart of the Victorian maritime empire. A young man of this district, if he did not actually go to sea, would likely be apprenticed to a seafaring trade.

Thus young Mullins and Uriah Mullins — whom we may presume to have been his father or other interested relative — have put pen to paper, and young William's future is settled. The self-discipline expected of an apprentice was strict, as the wording

makes clear: ". . . the said apprentice his Master faithfully shall serve his secrets keep his lawful commands everywhere gladly do. . . . He shall not waste the goods of his said Master nor lend them unlawfully to any. He shall not commit fornication nor contract Matrimony within the said Term. He shall not play at Cards Dice tables or any other unlawful Games. . . . He shall not haunt Taverns or Playhouses nor absent himself from his said Master's service day or night unlawfully."

In return for such fealty, the "said Master" contracted to teach young Mullins "the Art of a Sailmaker." Oh, yes—and to pay him the munificent sum of five shillings per week for the first year. This would go up at the rate of one additional shilling per week each successive year, until during his seventh year Mullins would rejoice in eleven shillings per week. (The shilling, discontinued as a unit of British currency in 1971, was equal to five pennies or ¹⁄₂₀th of a pound.)

Still, the apprentice *was* learning a trade—and this held out the hope of a better future than going to sea before the mast did. It also paid about the same, and was a great deal less hazardous. To quote from Greenhill and Stonham's *Seafaring under Sail*: "During the year 1876-77, 201 [British sailing] vessels were lost, taking with them 1,639 men. Seven years later, during 1883-84, 145 vessels came to grief involving a loss of 1,220 lives. These figures are quite apart from the very high losses incurred in the coastal trade and fishing fleet and among steamships."

So life was hard, on the sea as well as on land. The lot of the Victorian working class, the great mass of the population, was one of long hours, low pay, arduous labor, uncongenial and frequently unhealthy workplaces, and no protection whatsoever from the pitfalls of accident, sickness, or old age.

The one way a working-class or lower middle-class lad might rise above all this was to secure a good apprenticeship. Whether he chose (or was guided into) a shore-based trade, or went aboard ship to be trained as an officer in the merchant service, his chances were much improved. (As far as becoming an officer in the Royal Navy, he could forget it: that was strictly the preserve of "gentlemen." A lad of the working classes, no matter how talented, simply wasn't considered "of the right sort" to sup at a wardroom table.)

In fairness to the British nation of that time, the class system was thought to be the mainstay of social discipline at home and the pillar of the Empire abroad. This idea was generally accepted by all classes. It was only in the early 1900s, and especially during and after World War I, that these attitudes began to change. During the Victorian period, there were very decided rules about the relations between classes; one did not presume to ape one's "betters." It simply wasn't *done*, you see. And if you didn't like it, perhaps the only solution was to emigrate.

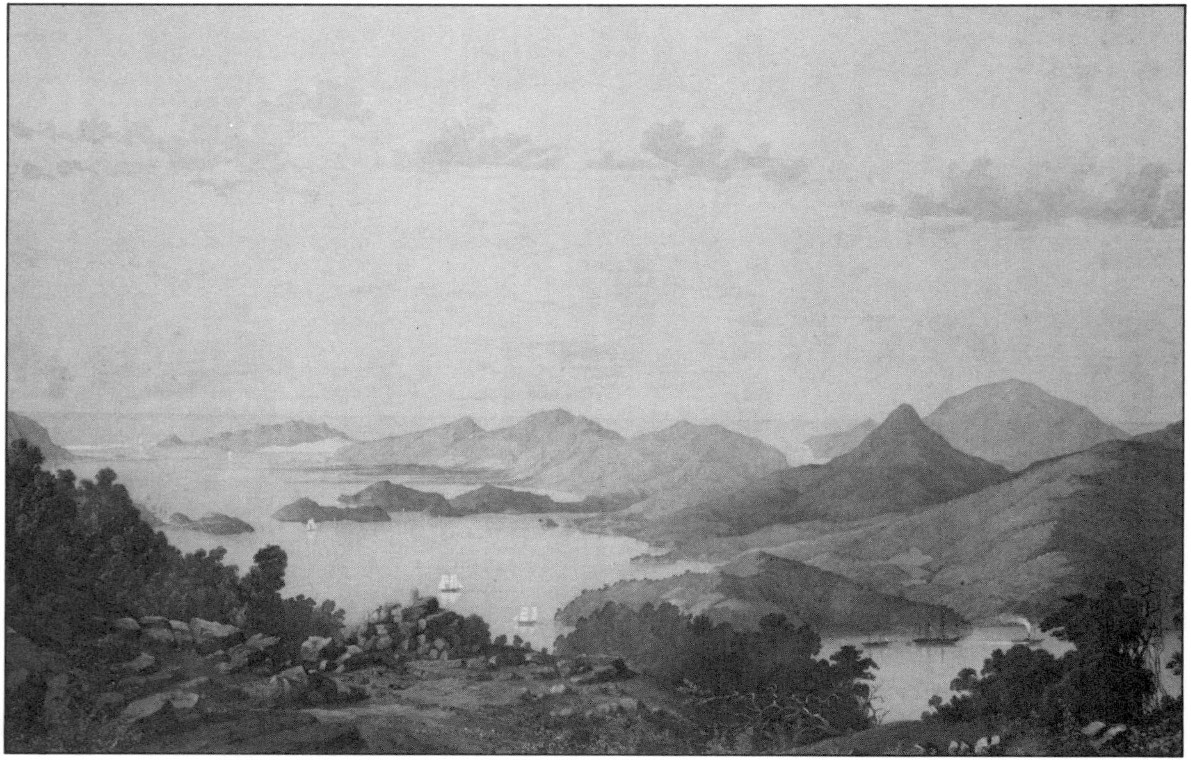

"View of Otago Heads and Port Chalmers" by George O'Brien.

* * * * * *

Mr. Paterson's Log at Port Chalmers[28]

Friday 1st Aug. 84
12.40 P.M. Came to anchor in 15 fts off Taiaroa heads to wait for water on bar.
7 P.M. Started & hove in short.
8 P.M. Tug Plucky came off hove up & proceeded in passing over the bar at 10 P.M.
11 P.M. Came to anchor in the stream abreast of Rocky Point mooring with 60 faths to SW & 45 to Norrd. Finished mooring at midnight placed D. Oliphant A.B. as watchman.

Saturday 2nd
Turned to at 8 A.M. and finished mooring. Got up all the steerage passengers effects & got them all sent ashore to the various destinations. Washed decks during the afternoon and finished up at 3 P.M. and gave the men the rest of the day.

Sunday 3rd
No work doing. Weather boisterous in the morning and hard frost towards evening.

Monday 4th
Started at 6 A.M. and rigged up gins & burtons etc. to discharge cargo with crew. Loosed all sail to dry and unbent them during the afternoon. Fine clear weather throughout. B. Johnsen sick off duty V.D.

Tuesday 5th
Started at 9 A.M. to discharge from after hatch into the Steam lighter "Shag" with all cargo for Dunedin. Working up to 5 P.M. Bosn with four of the crew sending down all iron gear for repairs

---

[28]Port Chalmers lies on the western shore of Otago Bay, South Island. It was a port for Dunedin up the bay, settled by Scots.

also royal yards. B. Johnsen sick off duty V.D.

Wednesday 6th
Started at 8 A.M. Discharging cargo with lighters on both sides. After Hatch Transhipment goods in Barge "Faithfull" & Dunedin goods in S.S. Shag. Finished loading the "Shag" at Noon & started the barge Thames. Boson with crew repairing damage done by lower yards coming down forrd. 2 hands repairing sails.

Thursday 7th August
Started discharging at 8 A.M. into Barge "Faithfull" on port side, transhipment goods, & Barge Thames on Starb side Dunedin cargo discharging spirits all day. At 10 A.M. the S.S. "Shag" came alongside & barge Thames hauled off to allow it to load. . . .

Her sides streaked with rust after a long voyage, *Euterpe* lies at an unknown wharf, ready to work cargo. Note how her fore and main yards cant in "cock-billed" fashion to serve as cargo booms.

Friday 8th
Discharging all day into S.S. "Shag" & Barge "Faithfull" all spirits from after hatch. . . .

Saturday 9th
Working at Cargo from 8 A.M. into barge Thames finished loading her at Noon, then loading Transhipment goods into Barge Faithfull up to 2 P.M. when the S.S. "Shag" came alongside with stevedores & a donkey engine. Had to stop to get it placed on board ready for stevedores to start work on Monday. Finished discharging at 4 P.M. then washed decks. Boson & his crew of three men washing, paint work, etc. during the day.

Sunday 10th
Fine clear weather continues throughout.

Monday 11th
Started with crew discharging into the S.S. Shag. Completed loading her & also Barge Faithfull. No stevedores at work this day. C. Nilson A.B. & W. Ek A.B. deserted.[29]

Tuesday 12th
Stevedores' gang of 6 men working main hatch into lighter "Trusty" clearing out Dunedin cargo from fore tween decks. Working after hatch with crew into lighter "Dorset." At 3 P.M. S.S. "Beautiful Star" came alongside & loaded with Tanks & general cargo for Oamaru.[30] S.S. Kakanui loading Invercargill[31] cargo at after hatch. Weather continues fine throughout. We this day finish discharging case whisky, all coming out in very good order.

---

[29]Desertion was common when a ship made port. C.A. Nilson and Wilhelm Ek, both 22, were Swedes.

[30]A town about 50 miles north of Otago Bay

[31]A town about 120 miles southwest of Otago Bay

Wednesday 13th Aug. 84

Stevedores' gang of 6 men working main hatch into lighter Shag, crew after hatch into Dorset. Completed Shag at noon.

P.M. Weather overcast & showery at 2 P.M. raining hard. Stevedores stoped as lightermen refused to work cargo in the rain. Continued with crew loading wire into Dorset up to 3.30. Finished loading her. Then started with crew sent down miz. topgt. yard and washed decks. 2 hands repairing sails. Found 18 drums of oil leaking some empty out of a shipment of 600 drums.

Thursday 14th

Crew working after hatch into lighter Anne Howlan. Stevedores working main hatch into lighter Trusty finished loading her at 3 P.M. and were then stoped for want of a lighter.[32]

Friday 15th

Stevedores working main hatch into S.S. Shag all Dunedin cargo. Crew after hatch into lighter Faithfull tranship goods. We this day finish discharging all cask whisky every cask turning out in good order no leakage. Stevedores stoped at 11.50 A.M. for want of lighters. Finished all Dunedin cargo into lighter Anne Howlan at after & main hatch[es] with the crew, during the afternoon.

Saturday 16th

Working out tranship cargo with crew, from the main hatch into the Lighter Faithful finished discharging at 5 P.M. then washed decks. . . .

Sunday 17th

Weather clear & fine with keen Frost during the night. No work started this day.

---

[32]One senses in this entry, the previous day's, and subsequent ones, Mr. Paterson's frustration with the Otago lightermen.

Monday 18th Aug. 84

Started at 8 A.M. discharging pig iron into lighter Faithful. At 11 A.M. the S.S. Kakanui came alongside and received the remainder of the Invercargill cargo. Stoped work the most part of the afternoon for want of a lighter, slight drizling rain all the day with NE wind.

M. Cotter A.B. and Collins A.B. deserted yesterday Sunday.[33]

Tuesday 19th

Discharging pipes for Bluff Harbour[34] into the lighter Thames clearing out all the large pipes that were at hand ready for discharging. Weather dull with heavy showers wind NE. At 3 P.M. S.S. "Beautiful Star" came alongside to receive Oamaru pipes finished loading her at 6 P.M.

Wednesday 20th

Discharging for a part of the day into the lighters Thames & Anne Howlan, finished up all Dunedin cargo that could be got at. . . . Crew clearing up the hold stacking wood etc. Lighters taken away to discharge into steamer.

Thursday 21st

Lighter Thames came alongside at 8.50 finished loading her at 3 P.M. with pipes for Wellington, Auckland & Bluff. Then discharged about 10 tons of pig iron into the S.S. Shag. Weather continues wet & unsettled.

Friday 22nd

Started discharging at 8 A.M. into the lighter Faithful pipes for Wellington & Bluff. At 11 A.M. the Steamer "Beautiful Star" came alongside. Hauled off the lighter and discharged 22 large pipes & 7 connections in all about 40 tons. Finished her at 2 P.M. then continued discharging into the lighter Faithful, clearing away

---

[33]John Collins, 20, had been born in Glasgow. Michael Cotter, 24, was a native of Belfast.

[34]Near Invercargill

the boiler for S.S. "Wakatipu" all ready to discharge.

Saturday 23rd
Stevedore Mr. G. Smith with crew's assistance rigging up purchase to discharge boiler using Double steel wire pendant from Main topmast head and Shored main yard with derrick using a threefold purchase on each.
4.30 P.M. Discharged the boiler into the S.S. "Taiaroa" then cleared decks & washed down.

Sunday 24th Aug. 84
Weather starts clear & fine. The "Nelson"[35] arrived today 100 days from London.

Monday 25th Aug. 84
Discharging tranship pipes into the Faithful for Wellington & Bluff also clearing dunnage in the lower hold.

Tuesday 26th
Discharging for a part of the day from 8.30 to 4 P.M. into the "Shag", Dunedin pipes & pig iron. Clearing up hold & tween decks when not discharging.

Wednesday 27th
Discharging all small pipes that could be got at in Main hatch finished them at 3.30 and was then stoped for the rest of the day. Waiting the Oamaru Steamer, crew clearing all wood etc. in hold.

Thursday 28th
Sent down the Main topgallant yard and at 10 A.M. the S.S. "Beautiful Star" came alongside discharged 28 large pipes & a connection, also 2 Hogsheads for Port. Finished discharging at 3 P.M. and was stoped again for the rest of the day. . . . .

---

[35]The iron sailing ship *Nelson* was built in Glasgow in 1874. Rated at 1310 tons, she became part of Shaw Savill & Albion's fleet in 1882. She was reported afloat in Chile in 1960.

Friday 29th
Discharged about 10 tons of Pig iron and small pipes and could
do no more as the large pipes were all in the way. Serving the
miz stay and sent aloft the crane of Fore topsail yard, also clearing all the Timeru cargo into the main hatch.[36]

Saturday 30th
No discharging this day waiting the Oamaru steamer. Crew
employed aloft at topsail trusses & parrels etc., also mending net-
ting round poop. Cleared decks & washed down at 4 P.M.

Monday 1st Sep. 84
At 10.30 A.M. the S.S. Beautiful Star came alongside, work-
ing at her to 10 P.M. discharging 56 pipes, also discharging into
the Faithful some Bluff pipes, and 10 tons of cargo into the S.S.
"Taiaroa."
D. Oliphant A.B. deserted.[37]

Tuesday 2nd
Started loading ballast at 1 P.M. loaded about 42 tons per
Result 22 & Henrietta 20.

Wednesday 3rd
Loading ballast all this day from Henrietta & Commodore
finished loading at 4 P.M. then trimmed it down.[38]

Thursday 4th
Discharging pipes into the Faithful & Trusty, all this day about
59 tons found a few small pipes crushed and broken in various
places in the wings.

---

[36]Paterson refers to Timaru, about 100 miles to the north.

[37]*Euterpe* had now lost five of her eleven A.B.'s to "run." David Oliphant, 21,
was a native of Montrose in Scotland.

[38]Loading ballast was back-breaking labor, every bit as arduous as loading or
unloading cargo. Too often, the sheer physical wear-and-tear on sailors *in port*
has been ignored by historians.

Friday 5th

At 10 A.M. the S.S. Beautiful Star came alongside and loaded to 2 P.M. 16 large pipes, then started to ballast loading about 47 tons per Rob Roy.

Saturday 6th

Discharging 1530 Bars iron for Timeru and 200 bundles and 3 tons pig iron into the lighter Trusty. Washed decks at 4 P.M. and cleared up for the week. 2 hands working at sails all the past week.

J. Baird A.B. when working at the pipes in the hold got his hand crushed, he is now under medical attendance and off duty.

Monday 8th

Discharging large pipes all this day into the lighter Agnes discharged 56 pipes. Weather very fine with moderate breeze.

J. Baird off duty with hand damaged.

Tuesday 9th

Discharged the remainder of the large pipes 18 into the Agnes and then a few Slings of small pipes in the Faithful but the wind freshening up to a gale and the ship tender, stoped discharging and started ballast at 2 P.M. loading 54 tons making a total of 223 tons. Boatswain & boy painting ships bottom.

Placed J. Baird A.B. as night watchman and returned the Bosn to day duty.[39]

Wednesday 10th

Loading ballast all this day per Don and Clyde 124 tons weather very fine & clear. Boatswain & boy painting ships bottom. Total of ballast on board 347 tons.

Thursday 11th

Discharging pipes from after hatch into the lighter Secret on port side and Faithful on starboard side. Also discharged a few Dunedin pipes into the Dorset at 4 P.M. The S.S. Star of the South came alongside and received a few slings of Queenstown pipes, also working the Lighter Faithful.[40]

Friday 12th
Discharging pipes all this day into the S.S. Star of the South on starboard side and the lighter Secret on port side.

Capn Hoyle & the Mate attending Court all the day on a case of Claim for drums of oil damaged, lost the case. Weather fine but sharp frost in the morning.

J. Menzies off duty having cut his eye with a piece of dunnage in the hold.[41]

Saturday 13th
Discharging into the lighter Secret up to 4 P.M. . . .

Sunday 14th Sept.
Weather fine & clear. Barq "Saraca" arrived 99 days from Glasgow.

Monday 15th
Pilot Paton boarded this morning to remoor the Ship after clearing hause hove in tight on the starboard chain and made fast again. At 11.30 started to discharge into the lighter Dorset . . . completed her at 5.30 P.M.

Loading ballast all the afternoon 29 tons per the Scotch Lass & Moa.

J. Menzies resumed duty again. Livingstone A.B. deserted.[42]

Tuesday 16th
Discharging from the after hatch into the lighter Faithful the

---

[39]John S. Baird, 22, was from Glasgow. Bo's'n William Collins, 35, hailed from Wigtownshire in the Scottish Lowlands. The "boy" referred to was probably an apprentice.

[40]Queenstown is over 100 miles inland from Port Chalmers.

[41]Dunnage consists of timbers used to brace cargo. John Menzies, 18, came from Dundee on the Firth of Tay.

[42]Malcolm Livingstone, 21, hailed from Ross.

remainder of the cargo. . . . Loading ballast all this day into the main hatch making a total of 449 tons. . . .T. Wilson A.B. started work this day.[43]

Wednesday 17th
Rigged up coal gear forward and ballast gear aft and started ballast at 10 A.M. Discharging coal into the Anne Howlan all the afternoon, weather dull & threatening. . . .

Thursday 18th
Discharging coals from Fore hatch all this day and loading ballast into after hold completed ballasting, making a total of 592 tons, completed discharging coal retaining about 10 tons for Ships use. . . .
J. Reid A.B. deserted.[44]

Friday 19th
Sent aloft the lower Foretopsail Yard but was unable to get it placed the crane not fitting exact. Sent aloft the main topgt yard. Fitted braces and all the gear for the lower topsail yard. Blowing a heavy gale from the SW with rain & sleet at times. When setting up the miz stay the band pin carried away again, sent it ashore for repairs.
Wtr Orbell A.B. started work this morning.[45]

Saturday 20th
Gale blowing with unabated force. Trimming down ballast and fitting gear aloft ready for sea. . . .

Sunday 21st Sep. 84
Weather clearing up a little heavy gusts at intervals. . . .

---

[43]Thomas Wilson, 25, was an Englishman whose previous ship was the notorious *Hurunui*—which nearly sank the *Euterpe* in 1879.

[44]John Reid, 30, had last shipped in the *Glengilder* of Aberdeen.

[45]Walter Orbell, 20, of Dunedin, had last shipped in the *Othello*.

Monday 22nd

Bent topsails, mainsail, foresail, main topgallant sail and jib, main topmast staysail. Fitted standard on fore lower topsail yard, and band for miz stay.

J. Smith A.B. at work this morning.[46]

Looking forward through the main and fore rigging, one can see how crewmen lay out on the yards to handle sails. Bracing their feet against footropes, they lean forward over the yards, balancing their bodies over jackstays. The old maxim was "one hand for the ship, one hand for the sailor." But in actual practice, both hands are often needed to haul up or loose the sails.

---

[46]"Smith," listed as "Scmidt" in the Agreement and Account of Crew, could not write and made an "X" for his mark. One suspects his name was actually Schmidt, first misspelled then anglicized by Mr. Paterson.

Tuesday 23rd

Started at 6 A.M. trimming down ballast and rove cat and fish falls etc.

8 A.M. Pilot Kelley boarded.

9 A.M. Started to unmoor heaving in the port chain at 11 A.M. hove the Port anchor up to the cat head, then hove away on Starb. to 25 Flhs at hause.

At 2 P.M. S.S. Plucky came alongside and at 2.30 hove up and proceeded at 4 P.M. with steamer alongside to Port. Passed the spit lt ship at 4.50 and crossed the bar at 5 P.M.

5.20 Pilot left, Wind from SSW dull threatening weather.
Ships draught
Aft 15/0 feet
Forrd 15/2
W. Donovan A.B., H. Wicks A.B. started work.[47]

9 P.M. Morrangi lt bearing W by N dist. about 15 miles, set the Patent log.

11.15 Light dipping W½S. Wind freshening up towards midnight with heavy rain.

---

[47]Both William J. Donovan, 20, and J.H. Wieck, 20, had come off the same ship as Walter Orbell, the *Othello*. Wieck appears to have had his name anglicized by Mr. Paterson, much as "Smith" had. Perhaps it helped when giving orders.

* * * * * *

FROM PORT CHALMERS TO NAPIER

From September 23rd to October 3rd, *Euterpe* made a voyage to Napier on the eastern shore of North Island. This town, situated on Hawke Bay, was a center for the wool trade so vital to England's massive textile industry.

The trip was fairly uneventful, except for a moderate gale that blew up early on. As always, *Euterpe* rode it out well. Later the winds left her just before Napier, leading Mr. Paterson to write "CALM" in large, frustrated letters in his log.

Still, the South Pacific must have seemed agreeable after the turmoil of the Southern Ocean. On the morning of October 3rd, the weather fair, *Euterpe* raised Kidnappers Point and stood in to Napier.

At the time of the ship's arrival here, the Maori wars which had torn the North Island for decades were ended, but the memories were still fresh. The Maoris, a Polynesian people, had not understood the white man's concept that by touching pen to paper, one could sign away a country. When this point was made clear to them, and after they had recovered from their astonishment, they launched a fierce guerrilla war that consumed hundreds of lives on both sides.

The British government shipped out a number of regiments to suppress the Maoris, among them the 65th Foot. From the Maoris' pronunciation of this regiment's number, the troops acquired their nickname of the "Hickety Pips." The skirmishes raged hotly during the days, but at night, Maoris would steal across the lines to inform their British opposite numbers that the Hickety Pips would be safe from attack while the sun was down. Apparently they always kept their word.

In the end, keeping their word did no good, and they had to submit to civilization's logic—Snider rifles and artillery.

After the Maori resistance was broken, the development of both islands began in earnest. The crown's sovereignty had been proclaimed in 1840, when there were barely 2,000 whites in the islands. By the 1880s, this number had multiplied to half a million. (Today the total population, European and Maori, numbers a little under three million.) Early on, the settlers found New Zealand's Scotland-like climate ideal for raising sheep. Wool became the major export. As soon as refrigeration techniques for ships could be developed, mutton joined wool in value. (The Albion Line's first refrigerator ship, the *Dunedin*, reached New Zealand in 1882.)

Thus, as *Euterpe* came to anchor at Napier, her crew prepared to load thousands of bales of prime wool to keep the mills of England humming.

* * * * * *

Mr. Paterson's Log at Napier
Saturday 4th Oct.
Hands employed clearing up the tween decks and hold ready for cargo. Carpenter at small jobs in cabin. . . . Placed the port pinnace in the davits for shore use & replaced the gig in its place.

Monday 6th
Rigged stages and started to beat & scrape the bulwarks & gunwale plate. Weather fine & clear throughout. Carpenter caulking Forecastle deck heavy surfe on the bar with very little wind.[48]

Thursday 9th
Blowing a brisk Gale from the Sthrd during the morning veering gradually to the Eastward with heavy rain. Strong gale towards noon from the ESE. At 2 P.M. paid out to 75 Faths. at waters edge, crew standing by during the afternoon, cleaning the iron work in fore peak during the morning. Gale blowing with great force, but backing to Sthrd. Officers watch kept during the night.

---

[48]The work mentioned here continued for the next two days. A sailor is born with a chipping tool in one hand and a paintbrush in the other.

218

Friday 10th

Gale moderated and clear weather. Chipping bulwarks & port plate all this day. Rigged up cargo gear at the main [hatch] and loosed all sails to dry.

Saturday 11th

Weather fine with a fresh southerly breeze finished beating the bulwarks fore & aft painting them two coats red lead. . . .

Monday 13th

Started to beat the 2nd & third gunwale plates starting forward, continued with all hands during the day. . . .[49]

Sunday 19th

Fine clear weather with light Sthrly breeze in the morning. The Second Mate with a crew away with the cutter fishing off the Pannier buoy.[50] A brisk westerly gale during the afternoon.

Monday 20th Oct.

Beating and scraping with all the crew and finished off at the quarter having cleaned the three gunwale plates & bulwarks all around. Carpenter repairing poop deck.

Tuesday 21st

Washing the paint work round house & bulwarks during the morning and painting the bulwarks & side the third coat of red [lead] during the day. Loaded per the S.S. "Sir Donald" 32 Casks tallow from Kinross & Co.

Wednesday 22nd

Painting side black & white first coat with 5 hands all the remainder working cargo, leveling ballast and assisting stevedores generally. Loaded 174 bales Wool & nine casks tallow per the S.S.

---

[49]The work of beating, scraping, painting and caulking continued the rest of the week.

[50]David Wylie, Second Mate, was 29 and a native of Glasgow.

"Weka." Mr. E. Smith, stevedore with 5 men at work stowing.

Thursday 23rd
. . . working at ballast leveling and dunnageing and otherwise assisting stevedores. Loaded 120 Bales per the lighter "Why Not", hove up about ten tons of rock ballast on deck to make room aft for stowing.

Friday 24th
Painting the port side a Final coat the boatswain & two hands finished up & started the Starbrd side. . . . Loaded 120 bales per the S.S. "Fairy" from Kinross & Co.

Saturday 25th
Painting the Starboard side a final coat from Forrd. to the gangway. Loaded one hundred & eighteen Bales & fifteen casks per S.S. Fairy. . . .

Monday 27th
Started loading at 6 A.M. from S.S. "Sir Donald" one hundred eighty-four bales, Lighter "Maid of the Mill" 150 bales & S.S. Bella fifty-six bales, crew heaving up ballast from after hold & assisting stevedores etc. . . .

Tuesday 28th
Crew started at 4 A.M. to heave short the chain. . . . At 3.30 P.M. started to heave up again and proceeded at 4.30 in tow of the "Sir Donald" ahead and the S.S. Bella alongside. Towed about three miles to the Norrd to the ballast ground and let go anchor in 12½ Faths water, 60 Faths chain at the hause. . . . Discharged the S.S. Bella when towing 56 Bales wool.

Wednesday 29th
Started discharging ballast at 6 A.M. with the crew and at noon the S.S. "Sir Donald" came alongside with one hundred & thirty-six bales, loaded them and continued at the ballast to 6 P.M.

Thursday 30th

Discharging ballast all this day to 5 P.M. when the S.S. Bella came alongside with eighty bales loaded them and continued at ballast to 5 P.M. when we finished discharging in all about 200 tons.

Friday 31st

At 6 A.M. Started to heave short. . . . At 10 A.M. hove up and set the Lower Topsails & Foresail and started away. At 11 A.M. came to anchor in a Foul berth a cable length off the "Wanganui", pilot berthing the ship, loaded 148 Bales. . . . At 12.30 . . . hove up anchor and towed into a clear berth. At 4 P.M. finished discharging the "Weka" 168 Bales, and then cleared the decks & secured the port anchor.

Saturday 1st November 84

At 6 A.M. discharging the lighter "Admiral" one hundred & eighty-four bales, and the S.S. Sir Donald seventy-four bales. . . .

Sunday 2nd Nov.

Weather very fine and clear. Mr. Almon ashore on leave, and boat out fishing, etc.

Monday 3rd Nov

Started and washed all the mud & dirt off the ships side and fixed the stages over the side to complete the painting. . . . Finished the topsides painting, scraping & beating round the stern during the afternoon.

Tuesday 4th

Loading from the Lighter Maid of the Mill . . . S.S."Bella" . . . and "Sir Donald." Some of the crew painting and stowing away the 2nd suit of sails into a locker that the carpenter has been eight days fixing on the port side of lower Forecastle.

Wednesday 5th

Loading 106 Bales Wool from the lighter Three Brothers, crew clearing out the ropes & gear from tween decks and stowing salt provisions in Fore peak. Carpenter repairing boat, etc.

Thursday 6th
Raining hard at intervals, awning spread over hatches. Crew clearing tween decks two hands repairing 2nd Mainsail. At noon the weather cleared and the lighter Maid of the Mill came alongside with 170 Bales. Raining hard during the afternoon. . . .

Friday 7th
Calm & clear in the morning. Painting the bottom colour with the punt & the boat. Boatswain with some hands sending up the new Foretopgt stay 2 hands repairing mainsail. Loaded 142 Bales from the Admiral & 109 from "Sir Donald."

* * * * * *

It went this way for *Euterpe* for the next three weeks, loading wool and patching up for the long voyage home. On the 11th, a fellow Shaw Savill ship, the iron barque *Pleiades* (1020 t.) came in from Port Chalmers. *Pleiades* subsequently transferred 900 gallons of fresh water to her fleet-mate. Alas, her career was not to be so fortunate as *Euterpe's*. On Halloween night, 1899, she was caught on a lee shore by a gale. Beached by her master a few miles south of Cape Turnagain, North Island, her crew got ashore but she broke up.

By Saturday, November 29th, *Euterpe* was nearly ready. It only remained to stow the last few bales of wool and whistle for a north-west wind.

* * * * * *

Mr. Paterson's Log at Napier
Saturday 29th Nov 84
Boatswain with crew geting ship all ready for sea. At 2 P.M.

the S.S. "Boojum" came alongside with live stock & stores & 4 Bales of wool which completed the Ship loading.[51]

2.30 Stevedore with his Gang left having finished blocking the main hatch. Sent down all the cargo gear and cleared the decks up.

Sunday 30th Nov
Light NE breeze in the morning gradually freshening, boat went ashore in the morning with 2 empty water casks. . . .

Monday 1st Dec.
Strong NE breeze continues no appearance of a change. Placed the cutter back into its place on the after skids & put the gig in the davits.[52] Geting all ready for sea. Carpenter battening down hatches, sent aloft main royal yard.

At 11 P.M. Pilot Mr. Kraafe came off wind having suddenly changed to NW.

11.30 Started to heave up wind gradually falling light.

Tuesday 2nd Dec
A.M. Heaving in and loosed all sail ready for a start. . . .
1.30 A.M. A light breeze came away from the NW, hove up anchor & made sail. When the anchor came atrip wind died away. At 2 A.M. a Brisk breeze came away from the Norrd which enabled us to reach out. When off the Bluff the pilot left. When the anchor came in sight found that the stock had parted & gone. Placed the anchor on the Forecastle & secured it. Wind light and unsteady towards 4 A.M. At 6 set the watches & hove the port anchor on the Forecastle & secured it.

Noon. Light Easterly breeze & fine clear weather. Standing towards Portland Island.

---

[51]*Euterpe* had loaded exactly 5,400 bales of wool and 56 casks of tallow.

[52]Mr. Paterson refers to a gig, a cutter and a pinnace. Gigs are the smallest of the three, cutters and pinnaces are of a somewhat larger size, and a long-boat or launch is larger still.

* * * * * *

FROM NAPIER TO LONDON

The ship was now homeward bound, eastward across the South Pacific to Cape Horn, thence up the Atlantic to the Channel. This final long leg of the voyage was comparatively uneventful. Thus we shall summarize it, with only a few of the more interesting entries included.

During the first part of this passage, *Euterpe* had the wind in her favor; she was still in the Roaring Forties, and the steady westerly breezes, interspersed with occasional squalls, drove her along at a good clip. On December 10th, she logged 185 nautical miles. On the 12th, she encountered a "Strong Gale & Heavy sea. Ship labouring & shipping much water." This blew over by the following morning, and *Euterpe* soldiered on from 50°48′ South, 153°9′ West.

She continued to hold the line of "Fifty South" as she ran eastward across the rim of the Southern Ocean. At times she would veer a few degrees to the north as gales and squalls buffeted her.

But then the winds ran out of breath. Mr. Paterson's entry for December 20th comments: "Midnight. Wind gasping. . . . Light baffling airs throughout." That day she made but 62 miles; the following day saw her gain drop to 28 miles. Mr. Paterson's largest script yet tells the story: "CALM; CALM".

The next few days showed little improvement (". . .sea smooth as glass. . . ."), but Christmas Day brought the gift of the wind's return.

In all these vast ocean wastes between New Zealand and the Horn, she sighted but two specks of man's existence on this watery planet. The first came on December 26th: "6 P.M. Passed a Schooner bound South on the port tack." This at 45°25′ South, 128°33′ West — or a little under 1,600 miles south of the nearest land, Pitcairn's Island.

"Thursday 1st January 1885" was boldly underlined and embellished a bit by Mr. Paterson. No doubt he had reason for some satisfaction at this point. "Bright clear weather" on this noon, and 185 miles logged in the previous 24 hours. A sickly crewman (Orbell) shipped in New Zealand was back at work. And *Euterpe* was fast closing the Horn.

January 5th: "Sighted a Barque on our port quarter. 53°47' South, 100°0' W."

January 6th: "Noon. Wind freshening to a Gale. Topgt. sails Jib and stay sails fast."

January 7th, 8th, 9th 10th: "Wind freshens to a gale. . . . Moderate gale . . . Squally . . . cold drizling rain throughout. . . ."

January 12th: "Strong breeze & Squally with mist & drizling rain. . . . Lat. 56°58' S. Long. 67°57' W."

And that evening: "Wore ship to the eastward. A heavy bank to the NW. . . . Wind coming away in gusts with slight rain. . . ."

At noon on the 13th, Mr. Paterson took his customary observations. The weather had cleared, and he found they'd reached 56°20' S., 62°47' W. Sailing from west to east in the middle of the Southern summer, the Horn had been passed with unusual ease.

After that, *Euterpe* climbed out of Drake Passage and worked her way up into the South Atlantic.

Monday, January 26th, found *Euterpe* about 1,400 miles east of the River Plate, still standing to the northeast. The day dawned peacefully, with a "light breeze from NW with clear weather." By noon, however, a gale arose and at 4 P.M. Mr. Paterson was recording a "Strong and increasing Gale & heavy sea, Ship labouring and shipping much water on the decks". By midnight, the gale abated and the sea was "going down fast".

Seven thousand miles away, at the confluence of the Blue and White Niles in central Africa, Khartoum fell to the Mahdi, and General Gordon died. But of these events, of course, the men of *Euterpe* knew nothing.

On to the north she went, her nose set toward England. By the 12th of February, she was in the Trades. On Wednesday, the 18th, she crossed the Line and met a friend. Exults Mr. Paterson: "Hove Ship to and boarded the Barque 'Ameer' of Picteu, from Cardiff to Batavia, received a quantity of bread & sugar.

After this convivial gam in mid-Atlantic, *Euterpe* slowly worked her way towards home. February passed into March, and *Euterpe* encountered more ships: "Sigld. the American Ship KCSL, 91 days from Astoria, Oregon, for Falmouth"; "Signld. the Ship 'Dolbardon Castle' of Liverpool, 100 days from Frisco bound for Cork." (Although averaging only 6-7 knots at this point, *Euterpe* had at last found a ship she could beat; she kept company with the *Dolbardon Castle* for two days, then pulled away, "gradually leaving her behind.")

Mr. Paterson busied the crew with sprucing up the ship, now that England was not far off. His log is replete with entries noting the "ratling down" of the rigging, painting, varnishing, scrubbing and cleaning. Brightwork was given a going-over, and on the 5th they "finished stoning deck fore & aft." The entry for March 6th contains an interesting note on *Euterpe's* paint job: "All hands painting the ships side black, ports, & lead colour down to the water edge." The next day, they "decorated scroll work round stern". This decoration is long since gone, probably a victim of the ship's later owners, the ruthlessly utilitarian Alaska Packers.

On March 21st, a sure sign of civilization appeared: "A large fleet of ships in sight *60*." The next day, 36 of these vessels were still in sight. Mr. Paterson does not tell us whither they were bound, but it seems probable they were part of the trade between Europe and North America, as the encounter took place at 45°N, 31°W, or pretty squarely into the transatlantic shipping lanes.

Euterpe was about to pay for her leisurely voyage across the Atlantic. For its size, the English Channel is one of the most consistently violent and unpredictable bodies of water on earth. On March 29th, the Western Approaches of the Channel welcomed *Euterpe* home in this way: "Wind suddenly chopped into NW and freshens to a Strong Gale. Furled the topsails. 4 to 8 A.M. Strong Gale with very heavy hail & rain squalls, sea rising, reefed the main & fore topsails & set them. Noon. Strong Gale with heavy squalls, Ship labouring."

March 30th: "Strong Gale with very violent hail squalls and heavy sea. Ship labouring and shipping much water on the decks.

A.M. Gale blowing with unabated force squalls increasing very heavy sea. . . . 8 A.M. Very Strong Gale mountainous sea ship labouring heavy. . . ."

March 31st (Mr. Paterson's last entry): "Strong Northerly gale continu . . . 4 P.M. Sea going down Ship labouring & straining. . . . 8 P.M. Ship lurching & straining very much. 11.15 P.M. Wind veered to NE. Weather clearing wore ship to the Norrd. and made sail. . . ."

Undoubtedly Mr. Paterson had his hands full from that moment on, so we must rely on Captain Hoyle to record the final days of the voyage. On April Fool's Day, they were forced to wear ship to the westward—losing ground in their battle to make the mouth of the Thames. Repeating this maneuver on the next day, by the 3rd they found themselves at 8°13′W—well out in the Western Approaches. Fortunately, the weather began to abate that day—only to do an about-face on the 5th and come back at *Euterpe* with a "hard gale (SSE) and thick rain". [Hoyle Log]

There followed three more days of knocking about, wearing ship and tacking again and again. At last, on the 8th, Captain Hoyle records: "Boarded by Plymouth Pilot boat and sent letters by him: Signalled off Prawle Point."

Captain Hoyle's Log
   Thursday: April 9th, 1885.
   1 A.M. Hauled ship by the wind. Thick weather & moderate Northerly to NNW wind.
   8 A.M. Sighted Isle of Wight bearing NE 10 to 15. . . .
   3 P.M. Tug 'Glen Lomond' came alongside—engaged him for £55 with second boat—if not required £50. Passed hawser to him and proceeded in tow.
   6.30 P.M. Passed Beachy Head: light NW breeze and misty weather.

   Friday: 10th/85.
   2 A.M. Received Pilot on board . . . and proceeded in tow.
   8 A.M. Passed through the Downs.
   6 P.M. Anchored at Gravesend.

Saturday: 11th.

8 A.M. Proceeded in tow and docked in E.I. [East India] Dock at 10 A.M.

Believed to have been the master's quarters on board the *Euterpe,* this cabin exhibits the Spartan accommodation which even the ship's commander knew. Here Captain George Hoyle may have passed many weary hours.

PHOTO COURTESY OF ROBERT SHARP

EPILOGUE

The mid-1880s seems like a suitable time to end this account. Steam was rapidly taking over from sail on the high seas — even on the longer routes. Shaw Savill & Albion kept the *Euterpe* sailing to New Zealand as late as 1897, but in order to compete with other lines, they, too, were forced to adopt steam and sell off sail. (This despite Walter Savill's personal antipathy toward steam — formed in the days when such vessels were mechanically unreliable and coaling stations few.)

As for the emigration trade to New Zealand, it tapered off after the boom years of the 1870s. For a time, those *leaving* the country almost equalled those still coming in. Instead of carrying hundreds of emigrants on their voyages out, Shaw Savill's ships now numbered their passengers in the dozens. The company turned more than ever to cargo — especially meat shipped home in new refrigerator ships — to take up the slack.

Yet sail, emigrants, and the *Euterpe* all had made an indelible impact on the new country. The sailing ship was the indispensable pioneer — the equivalent of the American wagon train — in the settlement of this remote, sea-girt land. The names of these ships — including the *Euterpe* — became traditional in New Zealand families, extending to the naming of infants.

It is with regret that the author ends the story here. He feels that he has come to know these Victorians personally — and hopes the reader has shared this sensation. In working through the documents they left, their personalities lived again. There was John Griffiths' onrushing, boyishly excited hand — while seldom paused for punctuation. There was William Paterson's steady, tightly disciplined script — with occasional large looping letters revealing tension with lightermen or light airs. There was Lillian Barry's homey hand — remembering back to the great adventure of her girlhood. This writer will always think of each — and all the rest — as individuals.

Today only one "individual" is left. That of course is *Euterpe* herself. In 1988 she will be 125 years old — and, as might be expected of one her age, she spends most of her time at ease. She still takes to the sea on occasion, however — and when she does, the sails are set and she bowls along with all the grace and gallantry she ever showed in the Roaring Forties or the Irish Sea.

In that sense, she remains timeless.

PRINCIPAL SECONDARY SOURCES

Bowen, Frank C.: *The Flag of the Southern Cross* (Volume I); London, U.K., 1939.

Brett, Henry: *White Wings—Fifty Years of Sail in the New Zealand Trade*; Auckland, N.Z., 1924.

Greenhill, Basil, and Stonham, Denis: *Seafaring under Sail*; Annapolis, Md., 1981.

Lubbock, Basil: *The Colonial Clippers*; Glasgow, U.K., 1924.

Lubbock, Basil: *Round the Horn Before the Mast*; London, U.K., 1911.

MacMullen, Jerry: *Star of India—The Log of an Iron Ship*; Berkeley, Ca., 1961.

Official Handbook of Ocean Travel, The; London, U.K., 1889.

Rogers, John G.: *Origins of Sea Terms*; Mystic, Conn., 1984.

Savill, David: *Sail to New Zealand*; London, U.K., 1986.

Waters, Sydney D.: *Shaw Savill Line*; Christchurch, N.Z., 1961.

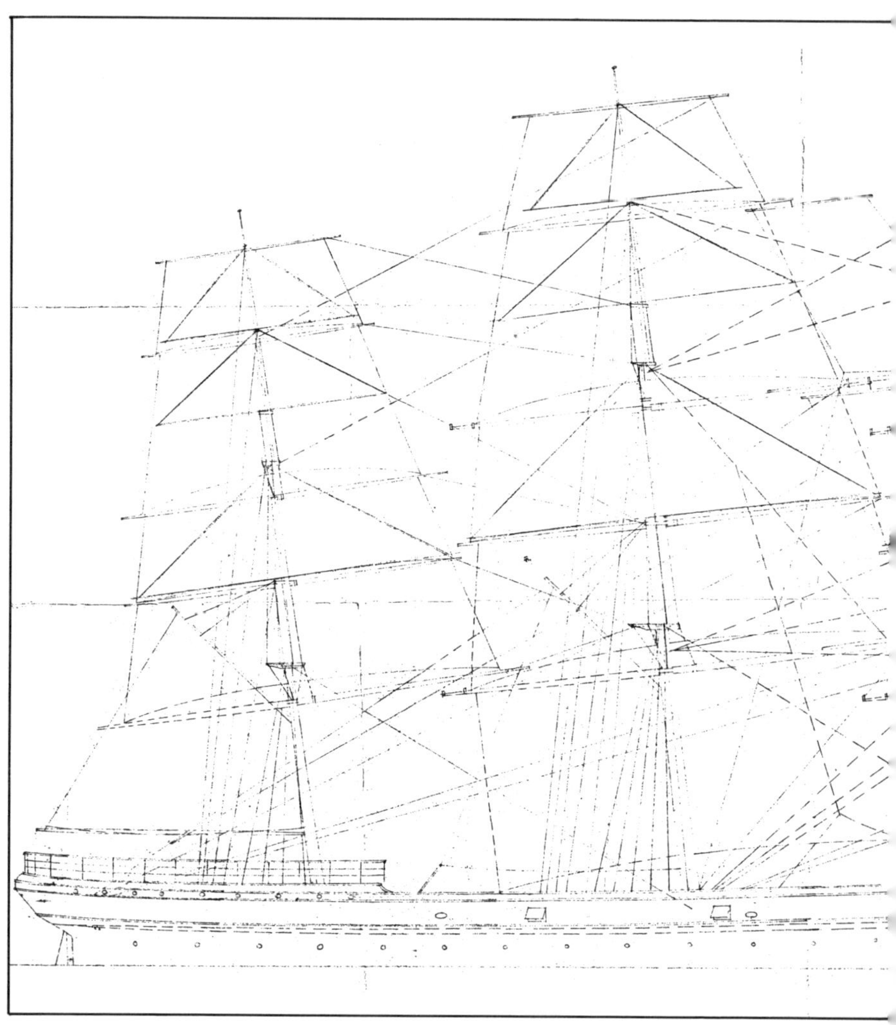

This sail plan of the *Euterpe* was completed by G.L. Watson on October 10th, 1872. Although faded, it shows the outline of the sails she carried in her Shaw Savill & Albion days. There is no mention in any known document of her setting studding sails or a spencer, as shown here, but Watson clearly allowed for that possibility. The headsails, those three triangular sails at the bow, are the outer jib, inner jib, and fore topmast staysail (from fore to aft). From the top

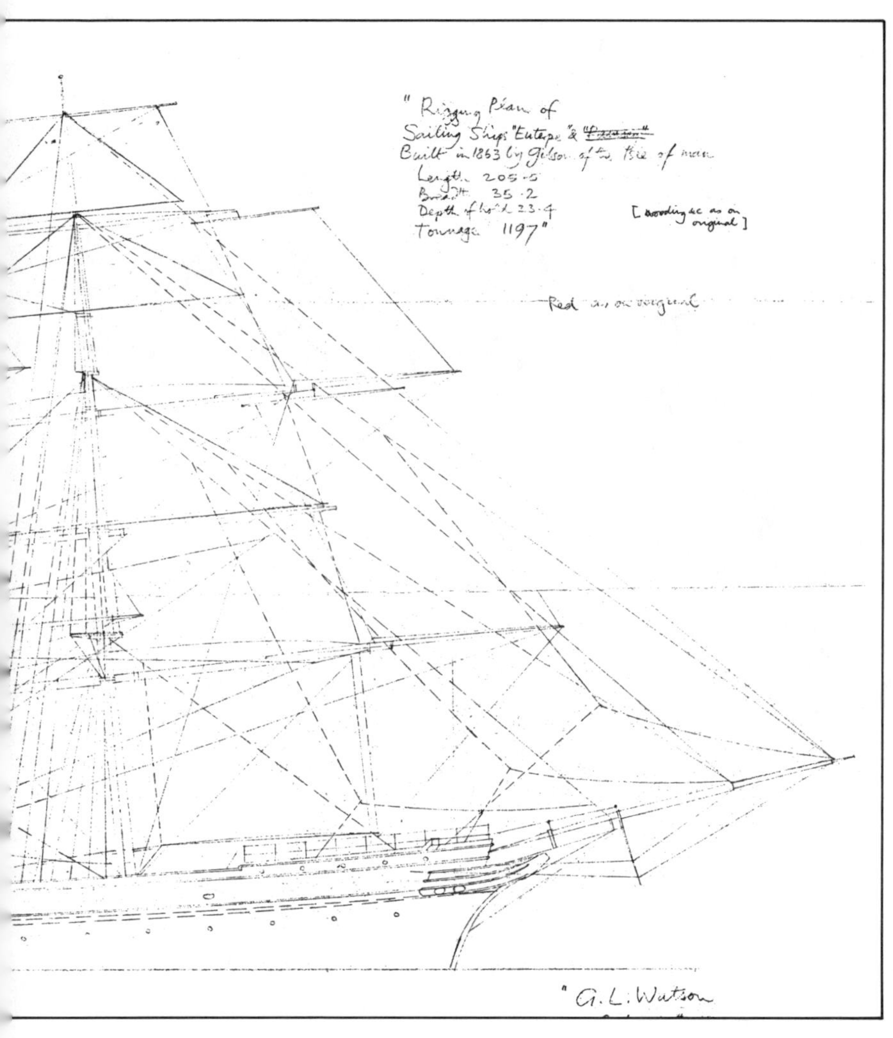

down on the foremast, we have the fore royal, fore topgallant, fore upper top-sail, fore lower topsail, and foresail. Between foremast and mainmast, the main topmast staysail is set. The square sails on the mainmast and mizzenmast are the same as those for the foremast, except, of course, they are designated main royal, mizzen royal, and so on. Not shown is the crossjack, the lowest square sail on the mizzen. The final sail, abaft the mizzenmast, is the spanker.

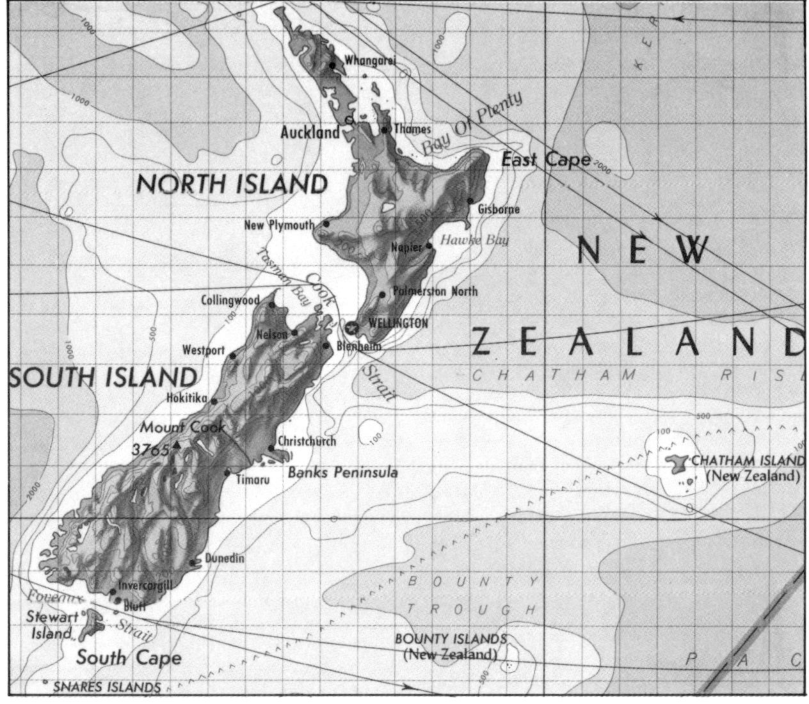

New Zealand, showing the principal ports *Euterpe* sailed to. Port Lyttelton is very close to Christchurch; Otago and Port Chalmers are in the immediate vicinity of Dunedin. On the west coast of South Island are the small ports of Westport and Hokitika, reached by John Griffiths in 1876. In the lower left corner are the Snares Islands.